BEYOND
ALT-RIGHT
AND
ALT-LEFT

A COMMUNITY OF
AMERICANS

OTHER BOOKS BY JOHN HOGUE

Ten Predictions for 2018 and the US Midterm Election Forecast
A Spiritual Rebel's Manifesto: Climb Aboard the Noah's Ark of Consciousness
The Great American Eclipse: Earthquake and Tsunami
John Hogue's Worldwide Astrological Predictions: Spring 2017 to Spring 2018
Trump Strikes Syria: North Korea?
President Trump Predictions
Predictions 2018-2019: Years of Crisis and Breakthrough
Nostradamus: Premonitions of 9/11
Nostradamus and the Antichrist, Code Named: Mabus
Ten Predictions 2016: The Fire and Ice Prophecies
The First Ever Nostradamus Prophecy Box Set
Everything You Always wanted to Know About 666, but were Afraid to Ask
Francis and the Last Pope Prophecies of St. Malachy
Prophecies for the Last Blood Moon
Predictions 2015-2016
The Essential Hopi Prophecies
A New Cold War: The Prophecies of Nostradamus, Stormberger and Edgar Cayce
Ten Predictions for 2015 and the Future of Richness
The Obama Prophecies and the Future of US Politics: 2015-2016
John Hogue's Worldwide Astrological Predictions 2015
Predictions for 2014
Predictions for 2013-2014
Nostradamus: The War with Iran
Nostradamus: The End of End Times
Messiahs: The Visions and Prophecies for the Second Coming
The Last Pope: The Decline and Fall of the Church of Rome
The Millennium Book of Prophecy
Nostradamus: The Complete Prophecies
1000 for 2000 Startling Predictions for the New Millennium
Nostradamus: The New Millennium
The Essential Nostradamus
Nostradamus: A Life and Myth
(ScryFy Short Story) Kamikaze Tomorrowland

BEYOND
ALT-RIGHT
AND
ALT-LEFT

A COMMUNITY OF
AMERICANS

JOHN HOGUE

BEYOND ALT-RIGHT AND ALT-LEFT
A Community of Americans
Published by John Hogue
Copyright © 23 October 2017 by HogueProphecy Publishing

Cover: John Hogue, Gail LaForest

ISBN: 978-1-387-47133-1

DEDICATION
To the pigeons diligently writing their commentary about human folly upon our statues, and who make their thoughtful "comment" on the cars of those who would tear those statues down.

ACKNOWLEDGMENTS
Thanks to my conceptual editor, Francis Perry, my copy and proofing editor, Gail LaForest, and thanks to Vipassana: a mother *once* and a meditation *now*, in *oneness*.

TABLE OF CONTENTS

FOREWORD
Documented Predictions
Of Approaching Political Crisis

This book is for the most part an anthology of editorially refreshed articles written in January 2008, February and September 2010, July 2015, September 2016 and recently from late August to early September 2017. Although lightly edited for better clarity, nothing of the details of what was forecast has been altered.

My own visions about America heading either for some kind of civil war or second and far bloodier American Revolution are among my earliest recorded. They first appeared in articles for *The Rajneesh Times* as far back as 1983. I have since collected and inserted similar visions in a number of books and articles written mostly by American seers of the past who share and detail a similar potential. Many of these are included in this book.

It took a while for US governmental attention to begin monitoring my forecasts on this subject. My phone didn't start

1

having that telltale "clicking" of a government wiretap until I did phone interviews in America, broadcast to the United Kingdom on several BBC radio stations in 1997 promoting *Nostradamus: The Complete Prophecies* (Element Books). The gist of my forecast was this: If the US Congress continues to sustain and intensify a partisan deadlock between Republican and Democrat legislators into the early decades of the twenty-first century there will be a Balkanization of America, either caused by a bloody civil war or revolution, beginning by 2020.

Balkanization defines a country or region undergoing a violent process of fragmenting into smaller and often failing states at odds and often at war with each other. I suppose my having stated that on a foreign radio show back in 1997 upset some suits and uniforms in the NSA and CIA. My phone remained click-click-clicking for another six months.

The clock is running down. I write this Foreword with 2020 only three months and two years ahead. I am sorry to report that the potential for civil or revolutionary war on the streets of the United States mentioned on BBC Radio 20 years ago is right on schedule with no moderation of the danger in sight. Indeed, the political polarization of America is now on steroids. The frustration of the American people grows. The bleeding off jobs overseas and the hollowing out the American middle class accelerates while it no longer seems to matter who citizens vote to represent them in Washington. Democrat or Republican, the candidates elected get there and quickly become worker bees for billionaires and corporate special interests. This is especially so since January 2010 when the US Supreme Court ruled in favor of Citizens United, effectively granting "humanity" to corporations, now defined as people and their bottomless pockets full of money called "free speech," buying off presidents and legislators. Citizens United has enacted the "golden rule" and Americans have lost their Republic to "those who have the *gold*—who now *rule*."

2

The free and independent press, a critical component to a Republic based on democratic laws is no longer "free" or independent. Rather it has become the "fee" press, dependent of corporate money. It became a ratings chaser starting 20 years ago when monopolizing media corporations started buying up independent networks. Now around 90 percent of all media in America is owned and coopted by six corporations. They have pretty much silenced real journalism that questioned power, now that power owned their cameras and could turn off their microphones.

The polarity of Congress I foresaw in 1997 has metastasized into a polarization of the United States, divided into two Americas, and tagged inaccurately as a red Republican conservative and a blue Democrat liberal. These labels are grossly simplistic. It would seem that the US education system, by stripping civics classes from middle and high school curricula for over two generations and counting is turning out political simpletons as future citizens. *Idiocracy* rules the day. The people are being financially and politically marginalized while America's government has turned into an oligarchic tool.

These are not unprecedented symptoms. They're just new to a nation that has taken for granted its freedoms and its citizen responsibilities to uphold and defend its freedoms from those in government no longer fearing the people rather than the other way around. When a power elite ceases to fear us, that is the prelude to revolution.

Before voices like mine are no longer wiretapped but potentially silenced or exiled, I will share with you my forecasts and those of others, which have anticipated these mounting dangers. I do this in the hope that the people of the United States will look beyond the polarity straightjacketing their minds and suppressing their basic sense of goodness, fairness, and tolerance for their neighbors. I hope this book can play its part helping all of us guide our political lives to a more positive future where Americans of all political persuasions can find common ground with each other.

Revolution is unavoidable, but what kind of revolution ultimately comes is definitely within our hands. It can be a revolution of free-for-all violence or a peaceful revolution and renewal of this nation.

This short book will help identify the dangers inherent in extremist Left- or Right-leaning identity politics and offer ways to make the coming revolution creative and peaceful.

CHAPTER ONE
Step Away from the Abyss
Of a Violent Second American
Revolution/Civil War

Where to begin? We are in for revolutionary times when the mad act of a man rendered powerless to effect change in his life, come to the end of his temper's tether, hurtled plane, body and soul into the black glass and steel face of an IRS building in Austin Texas back in February of 2010. Joe Stack had his 15 minutes of terrifying fame coinciding with an act in the US Supreme Court that effectively took the "Republic" of the United States away from people, handing it to monied, corporate interests. Twenty-eight days before Stack played Kamikaze pilot, the Justice John Roberts court moved five to four in favor of Citizens United against FEC. This ruling had inadvertently ended the Republic for which he, and 330 million Americans, should stand and defend from "enemies" foreign and domestic who happen to wear suits, buy off elections and politicians and hide their ill gotten gains in offshore banks.

In future times, 21 January 2010 will be the day remembered for setting into motion a corporate cabal where big, multi-national business became more "people" than real US citizens and their money became a more powerful tool of free speech than regular human beings could ever hope to use. The oligarchs had all the free speech money could buy with billions corrupting and influencing the people's representatives in office to take their money and follow their lead and forget doing the work of the people. The Roberts Court lighted the slow burning fuse on 21 January 2010 for either a future revolution and/or a breakdown of American society in a civil war by 2020.

What is more disturbing is that much of what Joe Stack said in his suicide note-cum-manifesto cogently and angrily touches on much of the discontent growing in America from a people feeling ever more disenfranchised and unrepresented by the US justice system and the Democrat-Republican duopoly in service of the new power in the world, the CEOligarchy. It is a new aristocracy where blue bloodedness was put aside for a black, bottom-lined definition of a human's "nobility" measured by how many billions one has acquired, hoarded and left stuffed away from money's main reason for being—creating a current, being a "currency."

Half of humanity's wealth is now in the hands of one percent of nearly eight billion souls on Earth. The tension that this creates between the haves and have-nots is breaking, all over the world and soon. When we enter the 2020s, civil upheaval will be the norm.

Later on the day Stack drilled the Internal Revenue Service building in his aerial assault on 18 February 2010, I wrote the following article entitled *The Joseph Stack Manifesto*:

***

I am a scholar of prophetic traditions. You might call me a historian of possible futures. There are a number of collective visions out there that, if interpreted correctly, point to revolution and even civil war in the streets of America no later than ten years from now [2020].

The act of domestic terror by Joe Stack was extreme. Moreover, today's violence unfortunately chalks up another successful prediction in *Predictions for 2010* I hoped would not happen. In Chapter 7, *Domesticated Terrorism*, I predicted the following, logged off on 1 November 2009:

I believe now the window of an overseas-based Muslim terrorist attack is closing as domestic jihad cells replace it. Added to this is a new terrorist danger arising in 2010. Not only from Muslims but white Supremacists, and right wing militias. The next great terrorist may be numbered among the angry and unemployable people who disbelievingly watch bankers and CEOs winning bonuses for busting the bank loaning payroll sustaining their jobs. The well-armed American unemployed go out to set a fire or throw a bomb in a CEO limo's direction.

What the first of these domestic terrorists states in Stack's "Stark" manifesto (below) are the very issues that may see the American middle class in the 2020s repeat what the French middle class did in 1789: initiate a very bloody and terrifying revolution in the streets of France. They had their own oligarchy of royals and aristocracy who did not listen to their grievances as they bankrupted France until at last when all posturing and talk of change was exhausted, the middle class of France led the masses into the whirlwind of the French Revolution.

Today's terrible act of violence—one man's storming of the Bastille with plane rather than pike and musket—could be taken up by masses of Americans in our near future. I fear that unless in the coming decade we the people can make our grievances understood in Washington D.C. we are headed for bloody revolution that will make the loss of life and property of the French Revolution look pale in comparison, and like the decade-long French Revolution, it can end in the fascist dictatorship of another Napoleon Bonaparte.

I said as much after appearing on Coast to Coast AM back on Tuesday night (27 January 2010) with George Noory as host. My three-hour interview, which you can download at Coast to Coast AM, took place later that night after I watched the narcissistic applauding and back slapping Congress root for, or roost grumpily against, an often toothy, Jimmy-Carter-grinning President Barack Obama giving his State of the Union speech.

Obama without shame reprised verbatim promises of change given a year before he failed to deliver. I said on the show that the president and US Congress remind me of king and aristocracy of Versailles, France, ten years out from the French Revolution, in a state of complete disconnect to their people's troubles, anger and the oncoming deluge of revolution. The US President, Supreme Court and Congress remind me of the Russian Czar in the first decade of the twentieth century giving words but little serious action to reforming Russia ten years out from the Bolshevik apocalypse.

Do not think it cannot happen in America.

Many prophets have foreseen it. On Coast to Coast AM I read a selection of their visions of the next American Revolution that we will go over, below.

I do not promote or wish to see this bloody future happen. The tragic act of Joe Stack, one software programmer/engineer who snapped, is a warning of what might come in ten short years if the invisible majority of suffering Americans should be left with violence as their only mode left to communicate to a mentally walled-in Washington D.C. adrift from democracy.

I pray for a peaceful Jeffersonian Revolution rather than the terror of the French Revolution, its Reign of Terror purges and the widespread massacres of the Vendee Civil War that followed between French Republicans and Monarchists. We must work towards a peaceful change as time is running out.

Here are extracts of what is purported to be the complete and unedited text of Joe Stack's manifesto, typed into the world before Stack left this world crashing into an IRS building in Austin, Texas:

If you're reading this, you're no doubt asking yourself, "Why did this have to happen?" The simple truth is that it is complicated and has been coming for a long time. The writing process, started many months ago, was intended to be therapy in the face of the looming realization that there isn't enough therapy in the world that can fix what is really broken. Needless to say, this rant could fill volumes with example after example if I would let it. I find the process of writing it frustrating, tedious, and probably pointless... especially given my gross inability to gracefully articulate my thoughts in light of the storm raging in my head. Exactly what is therapeutic about that I'm not sure, but desperate times call for desperate measures.

We are all taught as children that without laws there would be no society, only anarchy. Sadly, starting at early ages we in this country have been brainwashed to believe that, in return for our dedication and service, our government stands for justice for all. We are further brainwashed to believe that there is freedom in this place, and that we should be ready to lay our lives down for the noble principals represented by its founding fathers. Remember? One of these was "no taxation without representation". I have spent the total years of my adulthood unlearning that crap from only a few years of my childhood. These days anyone who really stands up for that principal is promptly labeled a "crackpot", traitor and worse.

While very few working people would say they haven't had their fair share of taxes (as can I), in my lifetime I can say with a great degree of certainty that there has never been a politician cast a vote on any matter with the likes of me or my interests in mind. Nor, for that matter.

Why is it that a handful of thugs and plunderers can commit unthinkable atrocities (and in the case of the GM executives, for scores of years) and when it's time for their gravy train to crash under the weight of their gluttony and overwhelming stupidity, the force of the full federal government has no difficulty coming to their aid within days if not hours? Yet at the same time, the joke we call the American medical system, including the drug and insurance companies, are murdering tens of thousands of people a year and stealing from the corpses and victims they cripple, and this country's leaders don't see this as important as bailing out a few of their vile, rich cronies. Yet, the political "representatives" (thieves, liars, and self-serving scumbags is far more accurate) have endless time to sit around for year after year and debate the state of the "terrible health care problem". It's clear they see no crisis as long as the dead people don't get in the way of their corporate profits rolling in.

And justice? You've got to be kidding!

How can any rational individual explain that white elephant conundrum in the middle of our tax system and, indeed, our entire legal system? Here we have a system that is, by far, too complicated for the brightest of the master scholars to understand. Yet, it mercilessly "holds accountable" its victims, claiming that they're responsible for fully complying with laws not even the experts understand. The law "requires" a signature on the bottom of a tax filing; yet no one can say truthfully that they understand what they are signing; if that's not "duress" than what is. If this is not the measure of a totalitarian regime, nothing is.

How did I get here?

First off, I will not make my readers endure Joe Stack's overindulgent and way-too-detailed tangents. So I will give an overview as I understand his ranting. Essentially his nightmare tale, starts in the early 1980s about being screwed one way or the other by a bureaucratically dense and uncaring Internal Revenue Service. He entered professional life as a trained software engineer thinking that 16 years of basic education from elementary school through college had him "pick up the absurd, pompous notion" that he "could read and understand English."

English 101 didn't prepare him for how words would be used by bureaucrats and the lawyer (liars) to obfuscate tax law into a turgid, incoherent labyrinth of un-clarity. He became savvy too late to the cunning way the government and corporations use communication to promote a nebulous smoke screen of words where the infamous "they" in power can screw the person of Joe Stack with their own interpretation of the law. Then, because *they* have the power, *they* forced him to blow his life savings over a few decades trying to legally fight the IRS and find a legal "interpreter" of Anglo-bureaucratese while the IRS garnished his earnings in one misunderstood tax penalty after another.

Apparently he got some bad advice. He started to play with "tax exemption" laws, like the Catholic Church had gotten away with. First big mistake. Second mistake, being above board about it. Very un-Vatican. Stack admitted that he took, "a great deal of care to make it all visible, following all the rules, exactly the way the law said it was to be done"—that is according to Stack's interpretation and not the government's. They ever ruled against his interpretation and he had to pay out $40,000 in back taxes to the Federal Government. More defeats were coming for this Don Quixote fighting windmills, or better, government windbags.

Long story made short, in his turgid rant itemizing the steps, the frustrations, the failed engineering ventures, the financial consequences of an emotionally difficult divorce, the economic strains of a new marriage took its toll. Add to that hard economic times finding work during what he called the economic "depression" in the early 1990s, the early 2000s. Play the working drone of drudgery. Endure 100-hour workweeks getting little to nowhere ahead financially. Then there was a move from Los Angeles California to Austin Texas, full of hope. It ended in bitter disappointment and further self-defeating fights with the IRS. It all made him one mad Joe, stacked with rage against the "the man" and his Federal Taxing machine.

Finally he had had enough:

I know I'm hardly the first one to decide I have had all I can stand. It has always been a myth that people have stopped dying for their freedom in this country, and it isn't limited to the blacks, and poor immigrants. I know there have been countless before me and there are sure to be as many after. But I also know that by not adding my body to the count, I insure nothing will change. I choose to not keep looking over my shoulder at "big brother" while he strips my carcass, I choose not to ignore what is going on all around me, I choose not to pretend that business as usual won't continue; I have just had enough.

I can only hope that the numbers quickly get too big to be white washed and ignored that the American zombies wake up and revolt; it will take nothing less. I would only hope that by striking a nerve that stimulates the inevitable double standard, knee-jerk government reaction that results in more stupid draconian restrictions people wake up and begin to see the pompous political thugs and their mindless minions for what they are. Sadly, though I spent my entire life trying to believe it wasn't so, but violence not only is the answer, it is the only answer. The cruel joke is that the really big chunks of shit at the top have known this all along and have been laughing, at and using this awareness against, fools like me all along.

I saw it written once that the definition of insanity is repeating the same process over and over and expecting the outcome to suddenly be different. I am finally ready to stop this insanity. Well, Mr. Big Brother IRS man, let's try something different; take my pound of flesh and sleep well.

The communist creed: From each according to his ability, to each according to his need.

The capitalist creed: From each according to his gullibility, to each according to his greed.

(Signed)
Joe Stack (1956-2010)
02/18/2010

***

My assessment of Stack's suicidal rant was published in a two part series at Hogueprophecy.com called The *Second American Revolution* with Part One and Two published on the 19th and 20th of February 2010. I'd like to add that the references to my appearance on Coast to Coast AM were recorded and listened to by an estimated audience of 15 to 20 million across North America just six days after the Supreme Court took down the US Republic with their ruling in favor of Citizens United:

The Second American Revolution
Part One

(Hogueprophecy: 19 February 2010)

As promised, I will share with you some of the prophecies I quoted on my Coast to Coast AM appearance back on 27 January 2010 that point to a future civil war or revolution in America. Seers such as Chicago based Irene F. Hughes have pinpointed that we will have a new US Constitution drawn up sometime in the mid-2020s. She did not mention a revolution taking place before this and I certainly hope we can come to this refreshing of American democracy through a measured and intelligent national debate and peaceful protest, if need be. Otherwise if the people grow more and more angry as their leaders advise caution and non-toxic dialogue while not <u>doing</u> or <u>accomplishing</u> anything beyond platitudes and talk, then the following future scenario described by these prophets below may be waiting to set fire to the land in less than a decade.

I present these terrible visions like one must sometimes open a wound to the air, so the festering can be exposed and healed, vanishing from the body of destiny because of our healing actions in the present.

The following passage comes from pages 183-184 of my book *1000 FOR 2000: Startling Predictions for the New Millennium From Prophets Ancient and Modern* published in 1998. (See *predictions*.)

***

Because our constitution is so inflexible, we will not be able to reform it. Instead, under the pressure of radical changes and perhaps a social war, we will adopt a new constitution.

David Goodman Croly (1888)

There will be great stress, as brother rises against brother, as group or sect or race rises against race—yet the leveling must come.

And only those who have set their ideal in Him and practiced it in their dealings with their fellowman may expect to survive the wrath of the Lord.

Edgar Cayce (1938)

Nation will rise against nation, kingdom against kingdom, states against states, in our own country and in foreign lands.

Brigham Young (d. 1877)

By the year 2026, the Constitution of the United States will be redrafted. The American system of democracy will be unrecognizable to that of the 1990s. But this will not be a negative change. Chicago psychic Irene Hughes predicts that man will live in greater trust and love of his fellow man at that time.

There will be an erosion and breakdown of the American Dream, says Edgar Cayce, when those who lead it proclaim their might and power as being right, when the leaders of this land have brought "many of the isles of the sea and many of the lands" under their influence. A second civil war will come at a time when America as the supreme superpower fears no man or devil. At that time Cayce warns, "in their own land [Americans] will see the blood flow as in those periods when brother fought against brother." (#2976-24)

In 1939, Cayce gave his future countrymen an alternative to civil war when he warned that if all Americans of every class and color didn't seek a "universal oneness of purpose" America would suffer a second revolution (#3976-25)...

In the 1870s, Orson Pratt, one of the early fathers of Mormonism, described the coming Balkanization of America would be a war pitting "neighborhood against neighborhood, city against city, town against town, state against state, and they will go forth destroying, and being destroyed. Manufacturing will almost cease, great cities will be left desolate."

John Hogue expanding on
what the seers said (1998)

***

Revolution is unavoidable but it need not be violent. Cayce has expressed the key to unlock a future where bloodshed on the streets of America does not take place. Protest need not be violent to be effective. We have Gandhi's and Nelson Mandela's examples in India and South Africa as proof that revolution can be far reaching through peaceful and patient non-violent protest and dialogue. In Part Two, I began a discussion with readers on these matters that have been ongoing for seven years by email or Facebook responses. The discussion began here:

The Second American Revolution
Part Two

(Hogueprophecy: 21 February 2010)

I have received many letters since I posted *The Stack Manifesto* on 18 February 2010 that express authentic anger Americans feel for their government (expletives included, vulgar as they are).

Anger must be expressed and released so that this poison is purged from the soul and clear-headed solutions and heartfelt compassion can resist, reform and revolute this nation. So, with that said, forgive my presentation of this very angry letter from "Chris." I will answer it in detail to explain why anger needs expression, but not as the engine of this revolution to come. Otherwise, with violent anger as the engine of the masses, the future will be awash in blood. This kind of revolution will lead ultimately to dictatorship in America. This land has another destiny in the Aquarian Age: to be the cradle of a worldwide religiousness, birthing an enlightened humanity.

Before demon-anger can transmute to divine understanding, let us examine a frustrated and volatile point of view many Americans share with Chris:

CHRIS
Live long and prosper, Joe Stack

HOGUE
Joe Stack will do neither. Perhaps it is true that we take with us beyond this veil of life what we identify with. As most of our identifications are unconscious, they may lead us like a magnet to a new birth into this misery-go-round Wheel of Samsara (wheel of unconscious life, death and reincarnation to new lives and deaths, on and on). In other words, if you live a slave of your anger, it will launch you into a new and miserable life framed by that anger. That is my sense of what happens as one who has faced death three times and possibly has had a glimpse of the other side.

I have come back from those experiences motivated to understand and thus transcend my attachments. Otherwise, I will return to my own soap opera, life after life.

I know the fires of profound anger. Joe Stack so completely identified with this anger that he committed an insane act of violence and now dwells between lives in the hell of his own making.

He is in limbo in the lower astral right now with only his anger and insanity as comfort. And remorse his only friend. Remorse for what he did to the gift of life given by existence and the gift of freely ending life that he perverted. In the future, a more evolved humanity chooses when to leave life. Only when life is beautiful and fully lived can a human being come to the pinnacle of life, which is death, and consciously choose that path. That freedom will be an inalienable right in the society of the new humanity coming. However in that equally free and responsible future, no one has the right to maim or take anyone else's life when you check out.

If Joe Stack had had enough, fine. Yet, Joe Stack burned innocent people and killed at least one person with his plane attack. I sense that he feels remorse for that now, and remorse for the wife and daughter he traumatized and left behind homeless by his own hand, burning down their house.

CHRIS
Joe is 100% correct. For all of my adult working life (40yrs) our self-serving scumbag politicians have benifitted more from the fruits of my labor than I did. Violence and revolt ARE the only answers.

HOGUE
The government is an expression of us. We are responsible for the government and politicians we elect. Even if you do not vote, you are allowing others to usurp their power by vote over you. The government is symptomatic of the collective health of a democratic society. The American Democracy at this time is adrift and ailing. Making the IRS or any other government body your boogeyman is throwing the responsibility away from the source of the problem.

You are all the problem, American people. You have the government you deserve right now. Change your consciousness and you will vote wiser governance in the future.

The Bolsheviks, Castro and his guerillas, Robespierre with his guillotine, agree with you, Chris. Violence and revolt are the only answers. Look what they gave us? An orgy of mob violence, the Great Red terror of Lenin and Stalin that killed 30 million people, the Great Terror of the guillotine that beheaded tens of thousands in revolutionary France. In the end, most of those executed were the revolutionaries who let slip the whirlwind, Joe Stack style. Violence as an end-all only consumes all that is good in the revolution as well as what it intended to overthrow.

Once this mayhem-mass mind has exhausted itself, do you think people like you, Chris, will be running the new America? Violent revolution will devour you as well as it did Robespierre, Trotsky and Kirov, even the ailing Lenin—who Stalin poisoned. The Stalins, the Castros, the Napoleons and the Hitlers step into the bloody void your mindless anger creates.

In Alexander *Soljenitsin's Gulag Archipelago,* he described a club of revolutionaries who wrote just like Joe Stack and you, Chris. They were believers in anarchic violence as the alpha and omega of answers to their grievances. They were thought to be even more radical than the Bolshevik Party and a greater threat to the Kerensky controlled *Duma* (Parliament) that took over Russia from the Czar in March 1917. When the Bolsheviks took down the Kerensky government in their Revolution in November 1917, guess who were the first people lined up against a wall and shot? That club of revolutionaries. That is what will happen to the future "Joe Stacks" if mad rage guides the next American Revolution.

CHRIS
And another thing, this country is literally crumbling around us. The federal gov't should be creating jobs to rebuild our bridges, roads, tunnels, dams and sewer systems. Its a crock of bullshit that there are not enough jobs to go around.

HOGUE
What you said here is true. These are the problems and our elected officials are not listening to us.

CHRIS
GW [Bush] has pretty much brought us all to our knees, and this new Obama-nation is following in his footsteps.

HOGUE
Yes. Obama is. I am aware many of you reading this don't like to hear that. I warned my readers as far back as March 2008, eight months before the presidential primaries for the 2008 Presidential Elections began, about electing demagogues who promise you every change under the sun. I was the first person in the world to coin the phrase *Obama Nation* in that article (see *Obama predictions*). He has come to his destiny too soon and too enamored with, and manipulated by, the American power brokers, lobbyists and aristocracy of CEOs and corporate moguls. There are great and tragic shocks coming to him that might get him back on track to his greater destiny. Right now, he is off track. That can change if your protest is intelligent rather than mindlessly violent.

CHRIS
When does it end? When is enough going to be enough? does it really have to come down to all us killing each other just to survive? This is supposed to be the greatest country in the world, to me its turning into just another third world country

too fucking poor to take care of its own. We import more SHIT from everywhere else because its too FUCKING exspensive to make here. Who are they kidding? I dont think there's enough people in this country to stand up collectively and say fuck you we have had it.

HOGUE

There aren't enough yet, but this smoldering mood you honestly and accurately express will spread. The masses of Russia felt powerless and angry, the masses of France did the same. When the critical mass of this suppressed volcano of mass anger reaches a boiling point in a country of 300 million possessing more than 300 million firearms, the revolution unleashed will be far worse than anything seen before on this earth. It will be a mindless blind rage of a monster hysteria swiping and destroying all in its reach: the guilty as well as the innocent will be carried off in the storm.

Revolution is destined to happen, but it is still in our hands to make it a peaceful revolution. We must move beyond anger and free all the genius energy anger devours so that the American people can think clearly, feel clearly, act by ballot and peacefully and courageously protest our grievances until our president, congress and court hear us.

First, find a way to privately express and free yourself from this anger. Don't be lost in the boiling rage of the mob mind. Were George Washington, Thomas Jefferson, Samuel or John Adams men who ran wild with their rage against King George's imperial taxation-without-representation machine? The founding fathers of our revolution were rational, cool, centered citizens. They tried in every way to find a peaceful solution to their problems with King George in the United Kingdom and only chose violent confrontation as the last resort. I'm hoping our leaders are not as stubborn and stupid as that mad king.

UPDATE 4 October 2017: *You, Chris, in your letter and Joe Stack in his suicide manifesto, promote violence as the first resort.*

Yet you on the red side of violence are not alone. The Conservatives have their nut cases, so do the Liberals despite all efforts of the more left-leaning US media outlets like MSNBC and CNN to downplay this fact and magnify Red Conservative malcontents.

I will take you forward in my narrative time machine four years and four months from February 2013 to 30 June 2017 when I posted an article for Hogueprophecy about the Republican Baseball Team Shooting. It happened on 14 June 2017, in Alexandria, Virginia. A Republican member of Congress and House Majority Whip Steve Scalise of Louisiana was critically wounded while practicing for the annual Congressional Baseball Game for Charity, scheduled for the following day. *The article then expands its scope with my assessment based on 30 years of first-hand experience into which side in this Red vs. Blue polarized political climate leaves more threatening emails in my inbox and Facebook pages.*

***

A testimony of one's accuracy in making forecasts about politics is the ability to eventually catch one's readers in the act of finding agreement for their political expectations from the forecaster. When you accurately predict every winner of the US presidential elections by popular vote since 1968, you have 13 chances to upset somebody and see how they handle it. Do they love you for one presidential cycle after predicting their candidate only to hate you the next because you predict the other side's victorious candidate?

Do they gauge how "brilliant" a predictor you are by how many times you seem to "agree" with their expectations, and call you a dummy (or much worse) when you predict the other party's candidate the winner?

To do this work accurately, you can't have a dog, or a GOP Dumbo or a DNC Donkey in this political fight. If you see the future you can pick up on the more evolved values potentially living in that future and adopt these in the present to predict outcomes of the present from a hopefully more enlightened, less identified mindset. That, I contend, is my open secret of accuracy. My personal expectations or those of my readers about the outcome do not blind me.

The 14th of June began with a session editing the passage I wrote a month earlier on Trump's 14 June 2017 birthday aspects for my new book *John Hogue's Worldwide Astrological Predictions for the Real New Year: Spring 2017 to Spring 2018*. But on 14 June, I had to put that book project aside and write about the karmic consequences of violent words, a lot of public frustration and anger, primarily coming from the left, and the Democrats. Namely, the rage mostly comes from those who just can't accept Trump is their president, after Hillary Clinton won the popular vote by 2.8 million over Trump but lost the electoral vote seven months ago.

I've seen a mounting, seething intolerance and hate. I've heard violent and even threatening words directed to Republicans and Trump from people in my blue-Democrat island village in the Pacific Northwest. I know first hand from direct experience with disgruntled readers that a majority of the most abusive and threatening letters I receive are posted by people wearing the mask of *tolerance*, the façade of being *progressive*. People who apparently on the surface, uphold a lifestyle of *non-violence* and *liberality*.

Mind you, I get a lot of abuse from people with all dimensions of political expectations my predictions accurately disappoint, but if I were to tally the vote of violent words aimed at me, I'm genuinely surprised how the emails and encounters with my liberal, non-violence touting, tolerant and progressive readers are far the more abusive and violent. Given the kind of comments spit in my face in person or blazing in my inbox waiting for me, fueled by the one-sided, daily harangue of MSNBC, NBC, and CNN reporting a clear and editorial-policy driven crusade to promote hearsay and outrage without sources, it is no surprise which side's handful of nutcases would draw the first blood.

It is no surprise in such a climate of mounting emotional hysteria coming mostly from the Left, that James Hodgkinson, a drifter from Illinois and a former Bernie Sanders supporter, fired the first shots of potential social war in a baseball field in Alexandria, VA. His target, Republican congressional legislators, lobbyists and staff practicing for the annual charity baseball game pitting Republican and Democrat House Representatives.

Now then, please count to ten, those readers who identify with the left. Stop shouting at your cellphone or computer screens at my words. Pause before unloading your bile and threats into my Inbox. I'm writing this essay out of love and compassion for you. I want to illuminate something that could take you out of a space of disempowering, media-manipulated emotions. America needs you on the left to calm down and wise up, so you can counter the era of Trump with better ideas on how to make America Greater or recognize how it is already great.

Consider the following, very public gestures over the past six months that have fanned the flames of violence leading up to the 14 June GOP baseball team attempted massacre on Trump's birthday.

Dear Democrat readers, did you ever see a world famous, mainstream Republican comedian of the stature of Tim Allen hold up a blood-soaked head by the hair belonging to Barack Obama?

Did you ever hear a world famous Republican-sympathetic pop star like Britney Spears or a well-known and politically vocal country music giant like Trace Adkins, step up before a national audience after Obama was elected—not once but twice—and do what Madonna did at the woman's march held the day after Trump was inaugurated?

There were small children in the audience who had to see and hear her hate and profanity. She started shouting long and hard "F*CK YOUs!" to people who voted Republican, then shared her dirty mental laundry about wanting to blow up the White House.

Have you ever heard Britney Spears, who was a supporter of G.W. Bush when he was president, or Trace Adkins, drop f-bombs into little girls' minds and threaten to blow up the White House because their candidate lost?

Since the election I've seen a California Democratic state congresswoman praise the vandals that broke in and tried to set fire to a UC Berkeley auditorium that dared allow a GOP lecturer from Breitbart News speak on campus. The left-wing answer to his opposing political views was violence and it was praised as something glorious, on the network news by that congresswoman on the left as a victory for free speech. Yeah, something those Nazi storm troopers did to people of opposing views.

There has been violence on both sides, and I do not give Donald Trump a pass on his violence baiting during the campaigns, but what about the left?

Consider the magnitude of the violent response to his encouraging isolated brawls with hecklers disrupting Trump's campaign rallies to what happened in a rally in Chicago.

Trump had to cancelled the rally to protect his followers because of all the threats of violence, but many had arrived already. The cancellation didn't stop the gangs from breaking into the auditorium, ransacking and beating dozens of people if they had a red Trump cap on their heads. It might as well have been a yellow Star of David, and the beaters might well have been Hitler supporters ganging up on them.

I don't have a dog in this fight, folks. That's why I may be best positioned to be a centered observer for a more enlightened, less politicized future and declare that the potential, pent-up rage was greater from the left, even before the elections took place.

Ever since Trump won I'm sorry to report that I've witnessed the lion's share of people being beaten up by mobs belonging to those wearing Trump red baseball caps on college campuses, freely practicing their First Amendment rights to peacefully gather and demonstrate in places like Berkeley, a university famous for establishing the Free Speech Movement in the late 1960s. It would seem that the Berkeley student body majority no longer practices the free speech that they once preached. The violence didn't stop with the auditorium's glass façade broken and arsonists from the left trying to burn it down because a Breitbart lecturer must be censured. Similar threats of violence have silenced other leading activists of the right, such as Ann Coulter, from speaking at left-sympathetic colleges.

You don't have to like Breitbart or Coulter, but in a democracy you do have to protect their rights to speak freely, if you expect that right for yourselves. Otherwise, how can you call yourselves Americans?

I've seen left wing counter protestors take cellphone pictures of students in peaceful Trump rallies on US Berkeley campus and then post them on information boards with threatening messages like, "Here are the new Nazis on campus.

KICK THEM OUT OF CAMPUS!" This is jaw-dropping behavior from a campus that birthed the "Free Speech" movement.

So now the first blood has been spilled, specifically and intentionally on President Trump's 71st birthday, 14 June, with an assassination attempt on Republican US House of Representatives playing baseball.

I blame the fueling-up of this sustained and rising intolerance on the anti-Trump biased media outlets like ABC, CBS, MSNBC, NBC and CNN. They have been fanning up the rage with a daily campaign to get Trump thrown out of office, playing up as of yet unsubstantiated claims of Russian hacking, then Russian collusion like we've returned to the hysteria and insanity of the McCarthy "commie scare" Era.

Russians are made the scapegoats for everything that left-wing people believe prevented Hillary Clinton from winning the election—except her dismal political skills. You'd think Russians today had become the Jews of yesterday in Germany. I have a large number of Jewish raised Democrat readers who just can't see the persecution parallel going on there. Didn't Hitler blame Jews for everything wrong in his Aryan German world? My Jewish readers, above all others, ought to recognize the latent anti-Semitism that has become anti-Russianism in this land.

I recall CNN anchor Wolf Blitzer openly musing on prime-time television a day or two after Trump's inauguration in January 2017 what would happen if the newly inaugurated President Trump, his VP Mike Pence and his key cabinet picks were all assassinated. He pondered about who then would pick the next cabinet and leaders and made sure anyone watching with an intention to do the president harm heard his rhetorical answer, the previous president and administration, Barack Obama, of course.

There was no reason to report such a hate-baited idea on national television to an audience already having their ears ring with Madonna's sweeping F-bombs and musings about blowing up the White House. CNN was feeding an urge to decapitate the US government. This was Wolf Blitzer spinning pure and potentially actionable, imagination. There was no plot uncovered by reporters to do such a thing. If there was, that should have been reported.

No, this was CNN shamelessly pandering imagined violence for ratings by fanning left-winged rage.

Now that they've pushed some nutcase over the edge after six months of this hate mongering and Russian fantasy conspiracy tales, does one watch a balanced examination on CNN about their own heavily biased reporting? That maybe their record-breaking surge in the ratings has a darker potential consequence?

The soul searching of CNN talking heads was subdued. Rather, the lion's share of their focused blame was still leveled at the president and his tweets. That's certainly a factor playing in this emotive mass-minded mess, but *really* CNN, rediscover a thing called journalistic *skeptical inquiry*...

I've watched the US news now for 54 of my 62 years visiting this world in a body-mind vehicle. I have never seen or heard a mainstream US news anchor before volunteer without prompting, what comes next after assassinating a newly inaugurated president and his cabinet. I can't help but think that this and other irresponsible reports have led to an assassin from the left casting a shadow on Trump's birthday, a disgruntled Bernie Sanders supporter, heavily armed, marching into a charity baseball practice. Upon hearing the ballplayers were Republicans, he entered the stands and began shooting US Congress legislators and staff members. He was killed in an ensuing gunfight only because a two-officer security team belonging to the third most powerful Republican Member of the House of Representatives was present. Otherwise, Hodgkinson might have massacred dozens of unarmed US congressmen and assistants.

Rep. Steve Scalise of Louisiana, the House of Representatives Majority Whip, was standing exposed out on the field covering second base, armed only with his mitt. He became the first shooting victim.

Scalise's critically wounded body lay crumpled on the baseball field while his Washington Police security detail waged a gun battle with the assailant. Other police units quickly arrived on scene. Together they helped shoot down and kill the assassin firing from behind the third base dugout. Ironically, that's the "left" dugout where the Democratic congressmen team would have sat if they were a visiting team at this baseball practice game. They had decided to practice on another field that day.

The gunman's other victims were Matt Mika, a former congressional staffer who also is in critical condition. Zack Barth, a congressional staffer for Rep. Roger Williams of Texas. Rep. Williams said to the press that Barth was lying in the outfield. "I give him credit. All the time he was bleeding, we were under fire. He was texting—he was texting, letting people know we were under fire and that we needed help. So, he's doing great. Vice President (Mike) Pence has spoken to him. I'm grateful for that."

Capitol Police agent Crystal Griner who battled the assassin, was shot in the ankle and is recovering in the hospital in good condition. Another US Capitol Police Officer, David J. Bailey, was part of Scalise's congressional security detail returning fire. Bailey received a minor injury in the gunfight and was released. Rep Roger Williams himself turned his ankle. This former minor-league baseball player has coached the GOP Congressional team since 2013.

I stress again, if the majority whip hadn't been at that practice game, the Democrat gunman, who got off 70 shots before police cut him down, might have massacred 20 to 25 GOP representatives of Congress who were only armed with baseball bats.

The charity game did go on, as scheduled on Thursday 15 June, in defiance of the hatred, and in celebration of America's game, as nineteenth century poet Walt Whitman once opined: "I see great things in baseball. It's our game—the American game. It will take our people out-of-doors, fill them with oxygen, and give them a larger physical stoicism. Tend to relieve us from being a nervous, dyspeptic set. Repair these losses, and be a blessing to us. "

My Democratic readers, dial this rage down. Don't dehumanize others by party label. Deal with your violent thoughts by doing cathartic meditation techniques, like pillow beating, etc. Vent your hysteria at a pillow, not at your fellow Americans who have different political views. It won't help them understand you if all understanding from your side is blinded by irrational rage and an inability to face the real reasons why your presidential candidate lost the election and it had nothing to do with scapegoating Russians.

My Republican readers do not meet this Left-wing rage with your own. Don't make this shooter a poster boy for millions of people struggling with their immaturity and anger over the presidential election result.

Today it's the left.

Tomorrow...? It could be your turn to collectively melt down. If Trump doesn't get his 62 million core voters all the things he's promised, especially getting many of them back to work or providing them a health care program that is better than Obamacare. If Trump is unable to make that happen, perhaps millions of you in red states will begin acting just like the Democrats behave right now. Then brace for your own version of James Hodgkinson. Let not a madman conservative paint all of *you* with the same bloody brush.

I've also been a target of your abuse and you have the potential to be just as dehumanizing of others with your labeling. Do not match violence with violence; or else it is all too predictable what can happen and it isn't good for the nation, good for its people, or good for the future.

On the Razor's Edge of War—PART TWO
Hogueprophecy.com 30 June 2017

***

Now we time travel back to the end of…

The Second American Revolution
Part Two

(Hogueprophecy: 21 February 2010)

Are we to follow the path of Usama bin Laden or Thomas Jefferson?

Let us choose to emulate people like Washington, Adams and Jefferson, over Robespierre and his guillotine, which in the end was used to cut off his own idiotic head to end the terror he started. Even the sixteenth-century French seer Nostradamus foresaw that end for such men when he said:

De gent esclaue chansons, chants & requestes,
Captifs par Princes & Seigneur aux prisons:
A l'aduenir par idiotz sans testes,
Seront receus par diuaines oraisons.

From the enslaved people, songs, chants and demands,
The princes and lords are held captive in prisons:
In the future by such headless idiots
These (demands) will be taken as divine utterances.

He wrote this in 1555 and indexed in Century (Volume) 1, Quatrain 14. By the way, the storming of the Bastille prison that started the French Revolution happened on the 14th day of July 1789.

I get where Chris is coming from [earlier in his expletive-spiced rants] because I share the same dominant ego identity trait. All egos or states of idiocy programmed over our souls possess one overriding trait. Some ego-idiot minds imposed on us are that of the Victim, the Narcissistic Bargainer (that's Obama), and the trait Chris and I wrestle with is being Anger types.

Strange thing about anger. When you are under its spell, actions committed in anger disempower you. Joe Stack's actions and domestic terrorism did not change a thing. The IRS goes on about its work now an ennobled victim. Indeed, his act of terrorism has indirectly branded all those with real grievances, like himself, with the same mark. There will be less listening now in the tragic aftermath of broken families—the surviving Stacks and Joe's victims—a burnt IRS office and a burnt home.

I can share with Chris and the rest of you meditation techniques that have helped me transform and free much of my life force that was under the grip of anger's tyranny. Just go to hogueprophecy.com and click on the "Contact Me" menu button, and put one word in the subject line: Meditation. I'll freely send you links and information to start your own exploration of meditations I utilize.

Free that liberated energy, then think, and feel clearly. Seek then creative solutions and be a part of a peaceful American Revolution.

About that revolution, I close with these two prophecies:

A body of censors will be created who will be responsible for policing the U.S. legislature at all levels.

David Goodman Crowly (1888), *Glimpses of the Future*

You are those censors and watchdogs.

In the year 2026, the constitution of the United States will be no more. In its place will be an entirely different document, and an entirely new way of governmental rule, I predict that man will live in greater trust and love of his fellow man at that time.

Irene F. Hughes (1974)

Meditation will be the cause of that happy change. Write to me and I will share with you those techniques that help me be a meditative revolutionary.

CHAPTER TWO
The Alt-Left:
A Spitting Image of the Alt-Right
Spilling Statues in Charlottesville

There are periods in the life of humanity, which generally
coincide with the beginning of the fall of cultures and
civilizations, when the masses irretrievably lose their reason
and begin to destroy everything that has been created by
centuries and millenniums of culture.

G.I. Gurdjieff (c.1916), *Meetings with the Miraculous*

A loving reminder: I say the following words with a peaceful
and compassionate heart. They are meant to help you. The skin
peeling of identity I am about to perform is necessary and
loving. If you read anything other than a state of even-
witnessing and quiet in my naturally descriptive and strong
words, then you are projecting your own suppressed emotional

issues upon them. Please remember that when reading the following article addressed to those in the world who would tear down statues and erase history in moments when these words might trigger something inside you and make further reading difficult.

Read on.

And if you see your anger rising, be a mere witness of it rising. It actually isn't "yours." Just watch thoughts, reactions and emotions, without being for or against them and over time you'll see them disappear as if you are a dreamer awakening from a long sleep.

What follows is a reality beyond wonderful.

Erasing history is not "learning" from history.

And yet, such acts of vandalism, whether by a government or an uninformed, hysterical mob mindset, are a common act at the end of great ages. A collective madness, fueled by a binary (0-1, black and white), intolerant and mediocre understanding of history fires the belly passions of the vacuous brained. Human beings become human "things" when they attempt to dispose of "things" that symbolize points of historical contention.

These "things" were once your neighbors, or your ancestors, represented in images and statues of the historically remembered dead. The historical literacy of those who would topple them seems to be as deep as the thin stain of pigeon poop splattering the statues. The intellectually challenged fixating on only one act of all-to-human error would topple symbols and overthrow the entire life and works of historical figures that helped our nation. All the good they have done is violently forgotten when mob-madness marches in the streets of Charlottesville, Virginia, on 11-12 August 2017.

It takes two to rumble. Left-wingers organized with their weapons of riot spoiling for a fight with right-wingers. The latter legally assembled in Charlottesville, a majority of which wished to peacefully assemble to protest the pulling down of Confederate statues of Robert E. Lee. No matter. Left-leaning ruffians sought out a willing minority of right-wing thugs in their ranks, equally armed, spoiling for a most unpeaceful assembly.

You young men and women on an anti-fascist crusade with sharpened fascist weapons in hand think statue crashing will clean the slate for righteousness by taking down General Robert E. Lee, just because you think he represents "only" a symbol of those who upheld slavery in the Confederacy.

Hold on a moment. Before you brain some neo-Nazi. Just how much do you know about the life and deeds of Robert E. Lee? Do you comprehend how citizens of America in those days felt about their states? That a man could defend his state from violent invasion as his reason and not in defense of slavery?

How many of you neo-Nazi baiters know that President Lincoln had sought out Virginian Robert E. Lee, the American Army's most gifted and respected officer, to lead Union forces to break the Confederate rebellion?

No memory spawns no virtue.

Be a force of mindless reaction. Hit that white guy with the Confederate flag while he's down, sprawled on the ground with your riot stick as photos of the Charlottesville riots show, even if the mainstream media fixated on the White Supremacists marching and Nazi saluting with Swastikas and Confederate Stars and Bars flags.

Tear down a statue of a Confederate soldier from its podium and spit on it like a barbarian from the Dark Ages or an Islamic State terrorist raiding an Iraqi museum to destroy statues of ancient Mesopotamian cultures.

Blithely have no clue how existentially torn Robert E. Lee was, a great and thoughtful man, when Virginia joined the

37

Confederacy. Lee rejected Lincoln's offer and joined the Confederacy not to uphold slavery but to defend his countrymen from invasion. Only a rampaging hooligan cannot know what country and people Lee was defending. Who wants to bother their pea-brained mind with the many shades of "gray" that brought good men on both sides to join the blue and gray armies on the battlefield of the American Civil War? Few of you hooligans give a hoot that many men of the South could not bring themselves to fight and kill their own people, their sons and brothers, their fathers.

You cannot rightly judge the past if you don't understand how people of the past thought and felt. Back in those days, your state was first your country, gathered in a union of other sovereign states. Lee could not bring himself to fight and kill his own kin, his own people, the Virginians. Therefore he could not lead the Union Army to quell the rebellion and he made the hard and terrible choice to defend his people.

Be compassionately advised, I am not defending the worldview of White Supremacists or the Confederacy. The Confederacy's way of life was based on the social cancer of slavery and it took a civil war to cut that tumor out of America and so far, not with complete remission. In the next three chapters you can read a series of articles I published in the hot and racially charged days of July 2015 that angered as many of my white racist readers as this article is upsetting my leftist-supremacist readers right now.

Perhaps it is impossible to reach my white readers harboring racist misunderstanding. I'll keep trying because I love them as much as I love my liberally unconscious friends. For today, I will entertain the possibility that there's the slightest chance that I can reach those of you who identify yourselves as being "liberal" or "progressive" by illuminating just how "liberal" and "progressive" you really are, or are not.

Then maybe you can love your enemies and have compassion for them.

When I see you behaving just like the people you hate, I see you becoming that which you hate. That's why I'm lovingly hitting you liberally-identified readers harder today. In a way, spouting liberal ideas but acting like a thug and a vandal of history makes you one thing the White Supremacists and American Nazis aren't, a hypocrite. We know where the racists stand. They show their faces openly at Charlottesville while the most violent liberals who clashed with them hid their faces like cowards, shrouded like ISIS jihadists do in black hoods—thug like.

Be advised. I'm about to use the word "idiot" a lot in this chapter. Before many of you on the left get your buttons pushed, please at least understand *my* definition of *you* as idiots. *Idios* in ancient Greek meant: *one who is under the illusion of being separate from the Cosmos*—the Universe. So, when I talk frequently about idiots for the rest of this chapter, I'm talking about people who righteously are under the illusion of being better, higher, more aware and more understanding than the people they are beating, and the people of the past whose statues they wish to destroy.

Let me say it categorically, *you are not any less of an idiot* than me or the other nearly eight billion idiots on this planet. Moreover, the difference between an idiot like me and you is atomically small. I am simply an idiot who is becoming aware that I'm under the illusion of being separate from the Whole. I contend that you are not aware of this difference if you are either siding with or running with those other idiots in Charlottesville who can riot because they have crystallized their illusion of separation from others in full-blown righteousness of ego. Who else but people who see the world through Identity politics can commit the acts of vandalism and violence I witnessed in Charlottesville? Why? Because the word "Identity" has its origin root in the word "Idiot."

OK, my fellow American idiots, here we go...

How many of you idiot Left Wing-nut Supremacists battling those other idiot Right Wing-nut Supremacists at Charlottesville demonstrations the other week know what important role of peace and reconciliation Robert E. Lee played in healing the nation after one of the most vicious and bloody civil wars in modern times? The vanquished Southerners looked up to him and he advised reconciliation and peace. If he had declared for guerilla war the South would have fought one.

By your acts you shall be judged by a cosmic intelligence that could be yours to awaken if you stayed your dark passions and opened your hearts to your enemies, as Yeshua (Jesus) did.

My God! Can you imagine Martin Luther King behaving like you have behaved in August 2017 at Charlottesville, you hooded and masked "liberals" tearing down statues like barbarians sacking Rome or ancient jihadists burning down the Alexandria Library in Egypt?

You were looters of history.

Martin Luther King used the greater power of peaceful civil disobedience and non-violent protest to move a racist nation a great step forward in civil rights for African Americans and the poor, a step that couldn't be achieved for a century after it should have happened at the end of bloodshed in the Civil War.

A peaceful man can move mountains of ignorance without toppling or spitting upon a single statue.

Do you think your violence will erase slavery and injustice from the world? Beware of your accomplices in history who acted like you do, trying to purge the world of people they judged hastily and stupidly as bad and evil, putting on airs of righteous purity they did not possess for it takes a monster to commit monstrous acts of obliterating history, thinking you are making a better world. What you are doing when you topple or remove statues is not standing with the righteous; you are standing with the Hitler Youth who gleefully burned books of Jews and intellectuals to purify humanity for a better world by attempting to burn their memories of Jews out with fire.

You idiots lobbying in Congress and in your assembled mobs on the streets now clamor for the removal of statues of George Washington and Thomas Jefferson from the US Capitol Building premises because they were slave owners. First it was the white supremacists marching in torchlight parades. In the future, you Liberal Supremacists will be raising your firebrands and like Hitler's barbarian children you'll someday storm and destroy the Thomas Jefferson Memorial.

My goodness, some of you have already defaced the images of Lincoln, the president who liberated the slaves, the president the first African American president loved most, Barack Obama. It seems you don't even know who fought who in the civil war. And then there was the VICE article online that had to change the original title of the article because some people were decent enough to complain. It presented an "Alt Left" title and theme: Occupy Mount Rushmore, South Dakota. It urged readers to wire with dynamite the faces of Jefferson and Washington chiseled on the mountain and blow them to bits.

I saw that kind of insanity committed in videos coming out of Afghanistan in early 2001 when the Islamic-fundamentalist Taliban decided to put on a big show touting their extreme hatred for any image of god or man as a sin of "idolatry." OK, fine with me if Islam as a religion doesn't want any images of the Prophet Muhammad or of Allah turned into statues or paintings, but where do you get off imposing your violent will on others who believe differently?

A thousand years before Islam reached Afghanistan it was a Buddhist nation. A sandstone statue of Buddha hundreds of feet high was carved in relief upon a mountainside, and up to 2001 it was one of the wonders of ancient Afghanistan. The Taliban videotaped it being blown to bits. They hopped up and down with glee, spitting on the rubble, and whacking it with their shoes just like I saw a mob of you *Liberal Supremacists*, gloating over a ruined Confederate soldier's statue that you vandalized in Charlottesville, glistening its twisted wreckage with your loogies of lustful anger.

I suppose a void of extremism must be balanced with more extremism. The "Alt-Right" must invariably go to battle with similarly idiotic people pitted against you members of an "Alt-Left."

Now we have emerging an "American" Taliban. I see the rise of an American ISIS, destroying statues of the past, objects to invoke memories of lessons learned and yet to be learned, thinking that wiping these things out, makes one a wise guy.

After the Buddha demolition, Afghanistan fell into darkness. After the book burning, the Nazis began to burn people. After the treasure trove of record of the classical ages was burned to the ground, people were forced to convert to a religion, not by love or by understanding, or a free heart submitting happily to God. No. With their heads forced to bow, covered in the ashes of lost classical memories, they were threatened to submit to a new god or face beheading by the sword.

It seems some of you sword bearers and library burners have reincarnated to herald and create dark ages again. When you erase a symbol of slavery, I assure you from understanding history's precedents, you erase a point of discussion and debate about ending slavery. I promise you, the day you destroy all the symbols of slave owners, wiping your mind blank of their memory, you will have hastened the return of your own slavery once again.

If you destroy the memory of Washington and Jefferson because of their one mistake, you have made their error more important than their many gifts to this Republic—gifts of freedom and an American dream given to *you* in humanity's greatest experiment in forming a republic with democratic values as the basis of its laws.

Remember what Yeshua said in the New Testament when a mob of men came to stone a prostitute?

"He who has not sinned, cast the first stone."

The original meaning of the word "sin" is to "forget" your divine nature. So I lovingly say unto you:

"He or she, white or black, who has not had a racist thought, cast down the first Confederate statue."

He or she, Caucasian or African American who has not hated, be the first man or woman to beat another flawed human *being*, just like yourselves. Use your club to hit someone sprawled on the ground in a mob riot in Charlottesville.

Your hand is becoming like the hand of ISIS. Today you break the statues with your hand-held hammers or use hands to pull them down with your ropes. Tomorrow your hand will grasp a knife cutting throats of the apostate un-American that doesn't measure up to your idea of being American, or you will use your hands to hang by the neck your fellow American with your grasped rope.

A savage paints the world in a black and white judgmental mindset of the mob mind. You will destroy the memory of Washington and Jefferson first, and then next you will destroy the US Constitution, the Bill of Rights, and the Declaration of Independence that they gave you.

I curse the unconsciousness of your enablers, the media anchors on TV whoring for news-tricks called "better ratings" while fanning your violence and witch hunts. I see a new left-leaning intolerance rising. It matches those on the extreme opposite and intolerant right.

There was rightful sympathy for the woman demonstrator at Charlottesville being a fatal victim of a right-wing hater, who drove his muscle car into a crowd of demonstrators, yet MSNBC's editorial filter throughout its hours of reporting in the aftermath never sought a balancing perspective. There was no mention of the well-organized Antifa hooligans enticing and inciting fights with the right-wingers. Left was lily white of any guilt. No caveat of a reminder was tendered for the equally hateful crime that happened a few months earlier when the Republican congressmen and their aids playing a baseball game were shot by a Left-Wing Supremacist in Alexandria, Virginia, simply because they were Republicans, as if your political persuasion collectively makes you a hated Jew in that man's blue-liberally fascist, worldview. Shall the world brand all liberals the same like I'm hearing news anchors brand all white people attending the demonstration with a collective and sweeping judgment?

One night after the riots, Rachel Maddow of MSNBC was leering with lustful glee at footage of men and women marching with backyard tiki torches in a rally to protest Confederate Statues being torn down. Yes, many of them were stiff-arming Nazi salutes and carrying stars and bars Confederate flags.

Guess what?

It is their First Amendment right to do so. The First Amendment defends their right to do it just as much as it defends your right to peacefully assemble and counter protest with your symbols of left wing pride, such as your LBTGQA rainbow flags. Most of the whites flying their Confederate flags are just as much against your lifestyle as you are against theirs, yet both of you, if you truly are Americans, must honor the First Amendment right of the other to peacefully assemble, period.

If you understand what it is to be a citizen of this nation, you must respect the rights of others as you expect your own rights to be respected. There are no two ways of behavior about it.

I don't support anyone's violent expression of their racial, spiritual or political "supremacy" over others, be it Right, Left, Conservative or Liberal supremacy—Christian, Buddhist, Islamic or Atheist Fundamentalist. Democracy is about living in community with others you differ with. Only a non-democratic mind, a totalitarian mindset, imposes its views violently to oppress and erase or destroy the lives of others. All who currently tear down statues and attempt to erase history are having their Fascist moment of unconscious action.

Rachel Maddow had her Fascist moment on air, using the power and responsibility of her television anchor position. She was goading her audience to recognize all of those white people in the footage of their peaceful march and get them fired from their jobs and branded as white racists "for the rest of their lives."

Rachel Maddow, you are a Jew. How can you hate and desire to hurt, and sweepingly brand all of those people for persecution, for loss of their jobs, meaning their children will go hungry and suffer?

Your judgment of them, your instruction to your viewers to persecute them and their families is you wearing your hatred and racism on your sleeve like the Nazis who forced your relatives to wear their hate on their sleeves from ghetto to gas chamber.

Your recent ancestors were forced to wear the Star of David that defined your people as subhumans to be denied jobs and persecuted in Germany.

Nazis lusted, *as you do*, for people of a certain race to be identified, stripped of a livelihood, their families to suffer, "for the rest of their lives" with no chance of redemption.

When you speak like that and incite millions of people watching to see those men and women's livelihoods destroyed, you have become allied with the very same darkness, once effectively goaded into action that murdered six million of your own people.

Be ashamed of your behavior and come back to the light of a loving heart.

CHAPTER THREE
Unintended Stealth Racism

I was surprised by the mostly positive responses to Chapter Two of this book when it first appeared as an essay posted at Hogueprophecy.com under the title *First a Word about Charlottesville and the Riots of Right and Left Winged Supremacists* (30 August 2017). The feedback had inspired my gathering an anthology of articles turned into chapters for this unplanned surprise of a new book. Thank you for the inspiration.

There was one commenter, however, that came to Rachel Maddow's defense in a way that, to me, reflects how an extreme ideological or religious point of view hides under the *blind* made of *slight*. I thank this man, who we'll call "the critic," for inspiring this next chapter.

The critic made the following observation:

"John, Rachel Maddow is from a devout Catholic family, not Jewish. She's a politics nerd, for sure, but don't dismiss her entirely—she has brilliant analyses at times."

To which I wrote back: "Thanks for the letter. First correction. I have not dismissed her; I'm trying to help her. Second correction: Rachel Maddow is actually a Polish Jew from her paternal grandfather's side. The family name was *Medwedof.* It was Americanized to "Maddow." Her roots come from the Jewish communities of the Galician areas of Eastern Poland during the Second World War years—a population nearly annihilated during the Holocaust. That's why what she said on television is so unfortunate and as dark as SS black uniforms.

"Rachel has fallen deep inside her own ideologically-hyper inflated narrative over the past few years. It's sad to see such a potentially intelligent individual surrender to the downward pull of stupidity's gravity. Authentic intelligence would not stoop so low. Real intelligence flies unidentified and un-Idiot-affiliated to any ideology because *ideology* rhymes with *idiot.*"

In his letter the critic suggested that Confederate statues and memorabilia should only be found inside museums. He rhetorically asked, "Does Germany have Hitler statues or Nazi memorabilia anywhere except museums? No. Our history should never be ignored or swept under the rug, hence museums dedicated to the Confederacy instead of outright devotion to a white supremacist/male-dominated machismo patriarchy ideology that many in the South hold so dear."

I replied, "No. Keep the statues up, because if people can be honest, they rarely if at all visit museums anymore. Our societies no longer teach us to make museum visits an important act of a citizen. We don't study critical thinking. We don't have civics in our high schools anymore. Such is the "Idiocracy" of our Democracy in present times. The people stumble like zombies to the threshold of a harrowing near-future peril.

"Beware of institutionalized forgetfulness. Better to have the Confederate statues in the parks, pushing our buttons, making us face the darker sides of our past and then have a discussion. And a word about Nazi symbols. It is a mistake of Germany to act like Nazis and erase those symbols. It is a bit hypocritical too, because those symbols show up in German movies like *Das Boot*, *Der Untergang*, *Die Brücke*, and hundreds of movies and documentaries constantly broadcast on German media. I think it is right that German media hasn't been forced to stop making films about Nazi times and hide its images and symbols from view.

"People make their symbolic gestures according to their convenience. For instance, if we take your logic to its crumbling conclusion, *Centrale* in Milan, Italy, the vast central railway building, should be demolished because Mussolini built it as a symbol of Fascist architecture. OK, tear it down. What then will happen to the Italian trains almost coming into Milan on time? I know what would happen. I've been through *Centrale* many times.

"Why not uproot all the autobahns if you want to erase symbols of Nazism completely? This first modern, interstate freeway system was one of the biggest achievements of the Third Reich. Even President Eisenhower modeled American interstate highway projects after Hitler's autobahns. German people, you don't want to see the statues from the Third Reich but you watch them on TV all the time and you enjoy Adolf Hitler's roadways to your heart's delight. Such self-serving hypocrisy, don't you think?

"I would say, let each city have a park in Germany where Nazi statues and symbols can stand in the light of day. Make sure they aren't tucked away, so people can't avoid the encounter with remembering. Showcase the Nazi statues in the biggest and most popular park in every city. The same goes for the Confederate statues in the United States. Not just parks in the South. Erect them in northern state parks too. Hoist on a pedestal Robert E. Lee on his horse in Central Park, New York City. No one gets a free ride to forget.

"Also, the Swastika is a beautiful and most ancient good luck symbol used by all ancient peoples around the world. Why should it be outlawed in Germany because of the crime of one man and one regime that so abused that magical symbol?

"What should we do about ISIS, the goddess, or children and businesses named after her? If you support erasing things from public sight, why not force all girls named Isis to change their names? Why not take down all statues of Isis? Should mass-mob ignorance hold power over Isis and the Swastika, and make them further victims of Islamic State and the Third Reich by legally suppressing such from mention or sight?"

The man defending Maddow wrote back a third time correcting himself about the MSNBC host not being Jewish. He did it in a way that makes me scratch my head in bemused bewilderment at how people can unconsciously say something that I'm sure, if they were more self-aware, they wouldn't utter. What the critic wrote next was latently racist:

"Rachel's background is indeed Jewish, but she's several generations removed to Catholicism and strictly identifies as such, as she has said several times."

To which with raised eyebrows I wrote back, "On one point I can agree, that Rachel Maddow at least in her mind, has identified herself "strictly" and only as a Catholic.

"That means she's got some issues about her Jewish genetic, cultural and religious heritage. She may be a 'Catholic,' yet every time she hears her popular Jewish name 'Rachel,' and every time she hears her last and americanized name, "Maddow," they are reminders that she comes from Jews. Catholics and other Christian sects by calling the Hebrew

Scriptures the "Old Testament" collude in an act of sanitizing their origin that is the *JUDEO*-Christian foundation of "strict" Catholicism.

"To me her strict identification for such illuminates why Maddow could say such hateful things the other night on her television show, that sounded so Nazi... or worse, so *strictly* and intolerantly *Catholic*. Here's why.

"The Church of Rome sustained a long and official persecution of the Jewish people for over 1,600 years. It fostered a Church-sanctioned anti-Semitism, spreading a climate of hate in Europe that eventually enabled the horrors of the Holocaust.

"It is an unfortunate fact that Catholic Church had spent 16 centuries branding Jews as "pernicious" and sealed it in Canon law. You couldn't be a Catholic without unconditionally accepting that Jews were responsible for the murder of Christ and therefore should be punished or forced to convert.

"Thus a long line of Catholic popes, presuming God spoke to them, created the realities of *Ghettos*. They forced Jews in the Papal States to wear the Star of David on their clothes to identify these "pernicious" lesser human beings, denying them equal status, denying them jobs, like Maddow encouraged her television audience to do to the Caucasians in the torchlight parade.

"If we are to stand as judge and jury against the latent fascism of those white folk in their Charlottesville torchlight parades, consider this. All the top Nazi leaders most responsible for the Holocaust as impressionable boys where indoctrinated by Catholic priests to honor the Church of Rome's fundamentally anti-Semitic worldview.

"Note the Catholic little boys who became mass murderers of those who murdered Christ: Hitler, Himmler, Eichmann, Goering, and so on. The little Catholic kid who grew up as Heinrich Himmler, the founder of the Gestapo and the SS, chose black for the uniform because it reminded him of those black-robed and "heroic" medieval Dominican friars who purged and burned Jews out of their towns.

"Pope Pius XII indirectly encouraged mass murder of Jews when he got on Vatican Radio after Hitler invaded the Soviet Union in June 1941 and blessed his invasion as a "Holy Crusade." He, like Hitler, also believed that Jews were a chief influence in the creation of Communism. This "Holy" Crusade killed five million Axis soldiers and civilians and 27 million citizens of the Soviet Union. This "holy" crusade's butcher bill included three million Jewish Soviet citizens, the lion's share of Jews murdered in the holocaust.

"It was Pope John XXIII who at last tried to break centuries-long and self-imposed *ex-Cathedra* laws institutionalizing anti-Semitism with no tolerance for questioning it. In Vatican II John erased "pernicious" from the prayer of the Holy Mass mentioning the Jews.

"So what you said about Maddow's often stated identification as "strictly Catholic" sounds to me like she 'has' completely converted to a suppressed fear and loathing of her own people, the Jews. She has apparently become that kind of Catholic that shies away from the "pernicious" origins of her family.

"It is therefore not surprising to me that she could unmindfully pass that self-loathing onto another group, like the Caucasians demonstrating with their Confederate flags and fascist salutes leading a television witch hunt, using the power of her TV pulpit to actively seek to destroy the lives of those caught on camera peacefully using their First Amendment rights. And I'll say again in Rachel Maddow's own words, branding them as racists 'for the rest of their lives.'

"Dear critic, I'm hoping you are wrong about her being that 'strict' a *Catholic*. The word in Greek means *universal*. Why therefore can't she be Catholic *and* celebrate her other religious and cultural heritage too?

"Before he became Pope John XXIII, Cardinal Roncalli worked as Papal Nuncio in France, Greece, Bulgaria and Turkey giving out Christian baptism certificates and passports to Palestine that saved hundreds of Jews from extermination during the Second World War. Maybe some of them are related to Maddow?

I don't know.

I hope she could become the kind of Catholic that Pope John strived to be when he asked for the Jewish people's forgiveness for centuries of strictly Catholic errors. In 1960, the year he proposed Vatican II, Pope John published the following prayer of atonement for 16 centuries of anti-Semitic Catholic polices:

"'We are conscious today that many, many centuries of blindness have cloaked our eyes so that we can no longer see the beauty of Thy chosen people nor recognize in their faces the features of our privileged brethren. The mark of Cain is stamped upon our foreheads. Across the centuries, our brother Abel was slain in blood, which we drew, and shed tears we caused by forgetting Thy love. Forgive us, Lord, for the curse we falsely attributed to their name as Jews. Forgive us for crucifying Thee a second time in their flesh. For we knew not what we did.'"

CHAPTER FOUR
Confederate Fried Myths
Of the White Supremacists
Facing a Black American Intifada

Two years before Confederate statues started toppling down in Charlottesville came the last wave of destroying Confederate flags in response to a white, right-wing mass murderer's action killing blacks in a Charleston church. Consequently, this resulted in a civil rights victory, long desired by African Americans living in South Carolina. To end the NAACP's boycott of the state for flying a flag in pubic areas symbolizing white on black racism, Governor Nikki Haley and the South Carolina State Senate approved the banning of Confederate battle flag flying above state capitol grounds. The following essays comprising chapters four, five, and six were written in July 2015, after witnessing the outrages of the white supremacist backlash across South Carolina and other southern states.

In 2014, I had foreseen such a dire possibility arising after an awakening in the black communities across America of what I envisioned would become a new Civil Rights movement. It was born in November 2014 out of police outrages in Ferguson, Missouri, that had escalated into a militarist invasion of this St. Louis suburb, populated by blacks overseen by a mostly white and prejudiced police force. When a white Ferguson Police officer was acquitted for shooting an unarmed black teenager a threat of demonstrations and riots ensued. The riot police dressed themselves like they were US forces marching down the streets of occupied Baghdad, to fire tear gas and volleys of rubber bullets against mostly peaceful demonstrators—fellow Americans—like they were foreigners to be subjugated by a police invasion and brutal occupation.

These standoffs with militarized police gave birth to the Black Lives Matter movement. I defined it as the American Intifada, because the street confrontations reminded me of Israeli military police in the occupied Palestinian West Bank territory mercilessly cracking down with rubber bullets and live ammunition against Palestinian youths armed only with stones and sling-shots. I soon found out that instructors from the Israeli police had trained many US policemen beating down protesters in Ferguson applying Palestinian-style riot control methods.

I foresee as a powerful racist-driven component from all sides in any potential future American Revolution and/or civil war. It is a demon this nation has yet to exorcise because it chooses not to completely and impartially understand what causes it and the depths of its influence upon American society, past, present and near future. Racism's Satanic hand guided the Southern states to defend an economic model based on slavery, requiring a civil war (1861-1865) that killed over 600,000 Americans. Yet before and long after that war, a greater holocaust was committed against the "First People," the Native

Americans, by European settlers actualizing their "manifest destiny," without a pause to reflect upon their inhumanity, striving to "tame" the Americas and consequently decimating the red, native races by the millions, nearly wiping them out.

Collective crimes of a nation can only resurface from the place wherein Americans suppress understanding what had happened and why Americans do what they unconsciously do. Without that understanding it is inevitable that racism will again play a fundamental role in any future social-civil upheaval of this nation. Such an insight awakened in my heart when I produced the essays in July 2015 that have become the next three chapters of this anthology on future revolution and civil strife in America. It is important to clearly illuminate these wounds. Expose them to the light for an airing of self-observation come what may filling my Inbox with angry and reactive emails—such as the examples you'll be reading below along with my attempts at a centered reply.

Now to the first of three essays:

"Oh what a loss in learning and letters!" said Nostradamus in his Epistle to Henri II in 1558, observing how people of modern times, despite their breathtaking inventions, many of which he foresaw, would often behave like functional illiterates. This prophet foresaw the invention of submarines, space travel, and a man landing on the moon and even the taming of electricity to make it speak on the very air itself as radio, television and your Wi-Fi. What is chest thumping on electric light and sound waves through the atmosphere and into our cellphones, radios and televisions is a whole lot of low-browed "loss of learning" drivel out of the mouths of mainstream mass media and pseudo Internet "historians" rewriting a history many appear to have never completely read. They simplify fact to promote the idea that the red flag with the diagonal dark blue cross studded with thirteen white stars is the national flag of the Confederate States of America.

Detractors call it a symbol of slavery and racism. Supporters—universally white Southerners—call it a symbol of a proud heritage of Southern Americans upholding states rights against federal tyranny. In either case, neither side seems to know what this flag they kiss or burn factually represents.

One thing it is not. It is not the national flag of the Confederate States of America. It was the "battle flag" carried by gray clad Confederate southern cavalry and infantry units in battles with the blue clad Yankee armies of the Northern states. So, technically speaking, what the organizations of white folk in the south claiming descent from those who fought in the Civil War are saying is in fact correct. This flag is a symbol of their heritage and their family's sacrifice on the field of battle defending their states rights.

Setting it factually straight what this ensign of contention was, we now come to the deeper issue. One that might spark a few truly hard questions about exactly *what heritage* were the Southern soldiers waving that flag for:

1.) What was your ancestors' *way of life* that was so threatened?

2.) Based on what socio-economic foundation, *without which that way of life could not survive* were Southern soldiers ready to soak their battle flags with their own blood and defend that way of life to the death?

I see a map of a ship with berths for "laborers" from Africa. Their places of rest, laid out on deck after darker, lower deck. Cordwood had a better bedding spot than this miserable human cargo, this fuel of flesh, blood and bone that ran the economic "way of life" of the South.

The South's cotton industry in the mid-nineteenth century was to clothes exports what Saudi Arabia today is for oil, "king cotton's" cornucopia where most of it was grown on planet earth. The crop was planted and harvested by an estimated one third of the total population of the Southern States, according the US Census of 1860, which was 9,103,332, including 3,521,110 African American slaves.

The past repeats its misunderstandings and mistakes in the future. The ancestors of rebel flag defenders today that mostly filled the Confederate armies were poor, white sharecroppers, most of whom couldn't afford their own slaves. They fought and they died by the hundreds of thousands for "the right" to become slave owners someday. They're just like working poor people of our times who will support political parties that defend the financial excesses of the modern gentry because they ridiculously hold onto a hope of someday becoming members of the wealthy class.

Now I hear my Southern readers about to have that cow over what I just wrote. Y'all please hold on, and listen. Here's the fundamental point that no protestation of states rights has yet answered adequately to my heart. Therefore, I give you all a rifled musket shot at it. In most cases this point isn't even addressed, perhaps because it is too ubiquitous to recognize.

The Sufis (Muslim mystics) say, "The fish in the sea are not thirsty." That's because they take for granted the all-encompassing reality of water through which they swim by which they breathe through their gills.

So then, my southern readers, I'm going to hypothetically take away your ocean, as it were, and lay the Confederate "way of life" high and dry on the beach in this following challenge. I'm taking away the ubiquitous thing through which your "way of life" swam, and breathed to exist.

Consider this.

What if Americans had no need for any business model requiring the requisitioning of a slave workforce? What if there were enough poor white sharecroppers, free men, to work the great plantations, which were the core of Southern culture and economic power? Specifically, what if the South had the same influx of free white men the North already enjoyed, filling their expanding factories, sprawling industrialized cities and manning the North's rich farmlands with an ample European immigrant workforce?

I'm talking here about an alternative future where no men in bondage existed in North or South. Everyone was free to work wherever they like and both Northern—and especially the Southern—ways of life in this scenario had bountiful European immigrant employees, therefore the South did not require a slave labor force to run the cotton mills and the plantations. I mean, one of the reasons why slavery rapidly vanished in the northern states wasn't because of noble designs of abolitionists. The immigrants flooding in made slavery an unnecessary economic expense because unlike the southern states, the northern states had ample manpower to fill their workforce needs.

Not the South. Their economic system needed slaves to sustain itself right into the 1860s, making their corner of America part of the last modern democracy on Earth that still kept slavery legal.

Now then, if in my alternative history of America there was no need to ship human chattel stolen from their homes in Africa to work your plantations, what then would be the mounting tension between North and South from the birth of America in 1776 to the early 1860s?

Would there have been a Mason-Dixon Line drawn so that all new states stretching west in the future should be divided into "slave" and "free" states as some compromise to keep the North and South in the union with two different "ways of life"?

Please explain how there could have been a problem, a division, a civil war between the North and the South if there had never been a need for one black slave from Africa to set foot on our shores?

The answer is simple, as it is categorical: the Southern states' rights depended entirely on an economic model that needed slaves to sustain itself just like a fish needs water to exist.

The abolitionists in the North and the anti-slave Republicans who voted in Abe Lincoln as president were a direct threat to the future of that "way of life."

Which brings me back to the Rebel Flag guiding Confederate soldiers into many a bloody battle of the American Civil War. It is a symbol of that way of life founded on slavery and thus it *is* a symbol of evil as much as it is a symbol of brave men who laid down their lives to uphold their state's right to become wealthy enough to someday buy and work slaves.

My Oracle accurately foresaw the police brutality tyrannizing poor African-American city centers is what brought this flag controversy to the forefront. It is an institutionalized atrocity fostered by another kind of racism, like slavery, that is, for many white Americans, living north or south, a "way of life."

Storefronts in Ferguson, Missouri, are boarded up as if this was Mississippi bracing for Hurricane Katrina. There is a hurricane coming to the ghettos in the inner cities and it may spread beyond what will be called the "Thanksgiving" Riots across America about to break out. November 2014's initial riots are just the beginning. In 2015 there will visit a nation-wide firestorm of protests that in the extreme future scenario could see black, Latino neighborhoods treated more like the ghettos of Gaza, and the West Bank of occupied Palestine. It will be called the American Intifada. Many lives will be lost and I only hope that what will be gained is AT LAST a serious civil rights dialogue that will end this plague of fatal shooting of citizens of color.

Ferguson Grand Jury Finding and
And the American Intifada
(Hogueprophecy.com, 24 November 2014)

My Oracle enlarged upon what that discussion and process might look like in a passage for *Predictions 2015-2016*, written six days later, on 1 December 2015. The brackets are inserted today for clarity:

Yet those responsible for dialogue will need to look at this police-versus-African American conflict in the three months of the Saturn-in-Scorpio final pass [June-September 2015] like [Martin Luther] King had once done. Racism is one dimension. Poverty, the other, and finally the militarization of domestic life at home. I foresee many policemen protesting against the Pentagon, imposing heavy surplus hardware on the shoulders of police departments. They might start finding common ground with those on the opposite side of the police riot line.

The direction of the dialogue and reconciliation will best succeed if it follows what Saturn in Scorpio illuminates: the economy (i.e. poverty), and what kind of inheritance will we give to the future (i.e. civil rights in a civil society). Invest in that future. Restart the war on poverty with money from a scaled down military budget.

The issue is this: Do we want to create an America divided by a new form of racism that defines equality and respect by who belongs to the "have-nots" versus the "haves"? Discrimination in the future reaches beyond the color of our skin. The balance in our bank account, or the lack of an account, defines our racial status.

Confront this issue now, or enter a decade of class warfare in 2015.

Predictions 2015-2016, Chapter Four:
All the Presidents Memes
(Subsection: American Intifada)
Parts of this chapter and much more appear in a shorter eBook entitled *The Obama Prophecies—The Future of U.S. Politics, 2015-2016.*

The Confederate army battle flag, since the civil war ended, has become the ensign of white racism for the Klu Klux Klan in the South, and other white supremacist organizations around the world. Moreover, as much as you white folks from the southern states would like to deny your red and blue banner with 13 white stars of all connections to black slavery, in a way, if you do, you are not completely honoring your ancestors who were Confederate veterans of the Civil War. There would have been no Southern "way of life" without it motorized by the bent, cotton-pickin' backs of people deemed less human than you.

Your ancestors knew that, moreover, they were proud to publicly defend slavery and their right of racial supremacy. Indeed, William T. Thompson, the designer of the Stars and Bars, the Confederacy's first of four national flags, pretty much spoke for many of the Johnny Rebs who marched off to die for "the Cause." He explained why his flag design just had to display a white middle horizontal bar.

"As a people, we are fighting [to] maintain the Heaven-ordained supremacy of the white man over the inferior or colored race; a white flag would thus be emblematical of our cause." (23 April 1863)

The flag Thompson is writing about was the Confederate States National Flag from 1861-1863. Other variants came afterwards that put the battle flag in the upper left corner of a completely white flag, standing for the white race. It caused problems though. So much white seen from a distance over a Confederate fortress or town looked like a white man's flag of surrender. A later edition in 1864 put a red strip on the white field's left edge to end the confusion and symbolize the sacrifice of a sea of white southern blood already spilled, as if the flag was reverently dipped in it, after three years of civil war.

When it came to blows in the 1860s, the final judgment on the South was delivered on the battlefield, for by then there was no other way for Yankee and Johnny "Reb" blooded white Americans to settle this matter. The South's greatest general, Robert E. Lee, interpreted the South's defeat as "God's will" that the South's way of life had to change and Americans had to come together once again as a united nation.

A few weeks after the war ended, Lee returned to the burned out shell of central Richmond, Virginia, the former capital of the defeated Confederacy, to pray at Sunday services held in St. Paul's Episcopal Church. An unheard-of thing happened. A young African American slave recently freed— and one might describe, joyful in the light of Christ—stepped up to the chancel bar to receive Holy Communion in the "whites only" section before the priest.

An audible gasp followed by a thick and seething silence issued from the segregated congregation, many of whom were wealthy white gentry and former leaders of the Confederacy sitting with their wives and families. In short, key members and former slaveholders of the ruling elite of the defeated South. All looked toward the minister who was stunned and didn't quite know what to do with the young black man kneeling on white church territory.

It was at that moment of high tension that Robert E. Lee, dressed in his grey suit, no longer adorned with a Confederate general's stars and insignia, rose from his seat in the back of the church and walked down the main aisle. All eyes were on him as he stepped up alongside the black man, and kneeled to take communion.

Historians from the North and South dispute what message, if any, Lee was making. Was it a proto-civil rights statement, by Christian action, accepting the will of God in defeat that required the white South move beyond its stance of racial discrimination and superiority? Or, was Lee for the sake of proper deportment coming to the aid of the perplexed minister to help the gentleman get on with the service and just passively and serenely accept the intrusion of the nigger. Just give him, give me, and the other waiting whites the wine, wafer and blessings of Christ and not make a fuss.

In my heart, the former is more appealing yet in either possibility Lee by his action that day was clearly saying to the aristocracy of the defeated South in that church, "It was time to move on and move forward." Change was coming. Be Christian and graceful about it.

We are entering another time of great change. Old icons, like the Confederate flag, are all becoming suspect and targets for iconoclastic acts as we enter a century of revolution. Be graceful as you move on. Never once disrespect those of the Confederacy who waved their flags crisscrossed by southern crosses on red fields charging into the flame and smoke of Union cannons and rifled musket volleys to their death and maiming. Honor these men, but before God, ask forgiveness from Christ for what these good men were fighting for, because *it was slavery* and *it was the evil core* of their way of life that led to a most terrible reckoning in blood.

So how can all Americans find an equitable solution to this flag controversy?

Seek to legally petition the taking down of any Dixie flags wherever they fly in the commons, in public places and government properties—state or federal—because white and black Americans share these. The same goes for the many state flags that, either with subtlety like Tennessee or brazenly like Mississippi, display the Confederate battle or national flag. That's the price the majority of white Southerners must pay for losing the Civil War and they must respect the feelings of a sizable black minority who are only living in this country because their ancestors were wrenched from their homes in Africa, naked and in chains, to work the white plantation concentration camps of America as slaves.

But I say this to young black men. I've watched you cellphone filming yourselves stealing Confederate flags from private homes. Don't go trespassing on people's property and stealing whatever flags they wish to fly there. Do unto others as you would have them do unto you, when you run up your banners to Martin Luther King, or the NAACP.

The American Intifada is entering a potentially more violent stage this summer of 2015 [when I wrote this essay]. Blacks have protested vigorously, making their point clear about institutionalized white police brutality and racism. Now there will come a white-supremacist terror backlash.

National reflection certainly has arisen since November 2014. The taking down of Confederate flags from South Carolina state capitol and other public places in the South became a catalyst for many black churches being burned across the South.

Upon reviewing my written material on the American Intifada, I came across my Oracle's future-dated time window for "massacres" of black men and women [documented on 17-21 November 2014] and it made me shiver on a hot summer's day in July 2015 when I was writing this essay. The focus of the following segment was on the future reckoning of police brutality causing an incident that could make Americans pause and reflect on the dire state of civil rights.

Here is that November 2014 passage from *Predictions 2015-2016*. Please note the underlined:

In the 1770s, King George III sent thousands of his red-coated riot-police "soldiers" playing cops, overly armed and cocked to "Ferguson" the streets of Boston. They lined up and advanced down the New England cobblestones as the monarchial establishment's occupying army to "restore law and order."

"Hands up! Don't shoot!"

Yet they fired on unarmed civilian protestors in what became known as the Boston Massacre—a watershed moment sparking the American colonial rebellion.

<u>You may have already seen such massacres of demonstrators by June 2015.</u> Certainly no later than that, there awakens a perception in the masses that the modern "redcoat" wears body armor and military gear. He rides in armored personnel carriers, and he sometimes shoots to kill citizens assembling in their streets.

Predictions 2015-2016, Chapter One:
The Stars War
The Empire Strikes Out
(Subsection: Saturn's Summer)

On 17 June 2015, Dylann Roof, a 21-year old white male, entered the Emanuel African Methodist Episcopal Church in downtown Charleston, South Carolina, shooting and killing nine African American parishioners, including the senior pastor and state senator Clementa C. Pinckney. Roof wounded a tenth victim who survived. The FBI recovered from his website an unsigned manifesto with Roof's racist diatribes against Blacks, Jews, Hispanics and East Asians as well as a collection of pictures, including an image of Roof posing with a handgun and the Confederate Battle Flag.

The slaughter of nine black people in the South Carolina church by a hateful white man who liked to wave the rebel flag—as it is often celebrated as a symbol of white supremacy—is only beginning.

Again, I ask young African American men, do not start vandalizing flags on people's private property and feed that hatred. You don't change hearts this way, you harden them. You are playing catalysts of reprisals. You are setting into motion very bad and potentially escalating karma. Stop it. Two of you have filmed yourselves. The World Wide Web knows who you are. So go to the police and under their escort and protection, take those flags back to their owners, apologize and reimburse them for any damages. Perhaps if you soften your heart you can soften the hearts of others.

Nonviolence means avoiding not only external physical violence but also internal violence of spirit. You not only refuse to shoot a man, but you refuse to hate him.

Martin Luther King, Jr.

CHAPTER FIVE
Slavery's Apologists and My Answer

My last essay on the Confederate Flag controversy stirred up a controversy of its own. So here are some of your replies and my responses that especially focus on a few readers who, I contend, have a seriously ignorant–though authoritarian–worldview on US history, slavery and racism that needs a compassionate Zen sticking.

I sometimes wonder if some readers' views on the pre-Civil War Southern way of life might be sourced to Professors Clark Gable and Vivian (Robert E.) Leigh from the University of cinematic *Hollyweird* magic rather than fact.

***

NANCY W.
What an Epic [last] *article, nice, truth, can't wait to hear all the feedback.*

HOGUE

Hi Nancy, and everyone. Well now, we start with… Gee, let me guess… A gaggle of white people either in denial that slavery was the core of the Southern way of life (a way of racism) or making some stabs at an apologia.

Let me say for starters that I love you all, especially those of you with your issues about reality, facts and the stain of some pretty moronic cultural programming brain-dirtying your minds. We come into the world as a *tabula rasa* (an empty page) that is blackened by the ideas, prejudices and identities of our parents, priests, politicians, pedagogues, pedophiles and pederasts of punditry.

I hope my compassionately-intended encounters below work in some way to provoke a good brain washing, if not in the people directly targeted, then for all of you reading this, whatever your brain-grimed background. So many people are afraid when they hear the word, "brainwashed." For one thing, they're misusing and misunderstanding the term when they see someone adopting some extreme ideology or theology like a stone-eyed cult worshipper. That guy's brain isn't "washed." He's just added a fresh pile of crap into his brain pan.

Why is it that people support hygiene for the body but not for their minds? You wash and groom your bodies every day, but leave your heads cluttered and accumulating refuse over an entire lifespan.

I'm all for washing my brain, moment to moment, because it has quite a talent for collecting garbage and making a personality, an ego, out of junk. I've found that Meditation can act like brain soap. You can simply watch the habit of soiling the brain with thoughts "washed away" by a moment to moment silence.

My words below, some of them scrubbing stained brains hard, many of them cold-water splashes of provocation, come from one who strives to wash his brain each moment so that some mystery beyond the brain's temporarily clean window can be glimpsed. Let meditation scrub the dirty screen of the mind and perceive something beyond the stain of identity called "John Hogue." Let it also wipe away momentarily the gathering grit of identities of all of you reading this. May you also discover what is obscuring the clean consciousness all of you possess: a sparkling and innocent intelligence beyond the brain that everyone is born with, but few ever clean their brain window to see "It." As my meditation teacher Osho once said, "We are born intelligent. Stupidity is borrowed."

Stupidity is the dirt we collect to clog our minds.

***

We begin with the first response, written in upper case to promote a shrill delivery, I suppose. Try not to trip over her spacing and backward opening quotation mark:

GENEVIEVE
YOUR STATEMENT, " STOLEN FROM THEIR HOMES IN AFRICA," does not identify their aggressor black brothers who stole them from tribes and sold them to buyers on ships. the buyers did not go deep into the African jungles searching and seizing slaves, they were abundantly supplied to the buyers for profit. that does not mitigate what happened to them by the white traders, but the whole truth should be exposed at all times.

HOGUE
Yes, it is true that African slave traders did the raids and the selling to the white slave traders. Just try to think this through a little deeper, Genevieve.

Be mindful, everyone, especially those of you who identify with your white skin color, that there's a habit programmed

71

into the mind by social conditioning that seeks to diffuse or deflect our crimes by saying, "Others did the kidnapping, I just bought them."

Yeah, what great African thugs our white American ancestors associated with. The true lowlifes who raided villages and dragged people away *to white men's ships*. There they were caught in the embrace of *white men's chains*. Why else would their abductors get paid dragging them all the way to the West African coast?

Clearly Genevieve is white. No African American, a descendent of slaves, would split hairs like she's doing. Anyway, if the first act in the outrage of slavery was bad, what the whites did to these people after the African traders passed them into their clutches is beyond terrible—the ocean journey on their slave ships. If you thought being a Jew in a Nazi boxcar train trundling down the rail to a death camp was bad (and it definitely WAS), consider the naked black men and women of Africa packed like cargo in the holds of slave ships. They were handed over to white slavers—stolen, Genevieve—from their continent by *our* American white folk armed with guns and whips.

The whites were shackling their cargo on pallets with nary inches of space to breathe, stuffed beneath the next pallet and the next. Stack after stack of Africans laid into them, hardly able to move or breath, all spewing their diarrhea and sea sickness puke from top pallets to bottom—down, down, trickling down uneconomically, it goes: the filth of human horror and misery.

Could Dante's inferno be any worse?

Most of the weeks or months of the ocean journey were spent laid out like cordwood below decks in that stygian stench and the tropical heat. It was so bad that during brief exercise sessions above deck, some slaves broke free and plunged over the side. Death and drowning by the weight of their chains was better than living like that.

So Genevieve, I do take note and amend my article with the above and say to you, yes, African black and Muslim Arab brown raiders committed the first crime. They did it because the primary criminals were the white slavers making the human trafficking business possible and profitable. The white slave traders remain—as I wrote—those who stole black people out of Africa in their Black Holocaust fleets of misery and horror. The journey's end for the survivors was slavery—period. You can't skirt this truth or dodge the blame.

***

Here is another Confederate apologist.

R.C.C.
Hey Johnny, you're story needs a little more research. You omitted Camp Dexter, the most notorious torture complex in the history of humanity, Honest Abe turned a blind-eye too all types of medical experiments, electro-shock submission and, this just skims the surface !!!!!

HOGUE
You can use your exclamation marks to the point of disempowerment all you want, R.C.C. and cry me a river all the way to the Andersonville prisoner of war concentration camp holding Union POWs. Here's why. Like Genevieve, you are trying to turn attention away from the South's crimes against humanity by pointing the finger at "honest Abe" and his crimes. That doesn't wash with me. If I murder somebody and point at another murderer... What? You think my murderous act just disappears? You are avoiding my point because you don't want to face it full on.

Racism in this country is deep northern and deep southern, then as now. A whole lot of people in the North didn't care about Lincoln's Emancipation Proclamation, either. They also saw this as a states' rights versus union matter first. It is a testimony to Lincoln's evolution as a human being that he came to understand the heart of the issue that most Union and certainly most Confederates hadn't the genius or wisdom to confront. Slavery is the core of the Southern, plantation-slave labor economic model. Otherwise, as my [last chapter] stated comprehensively—to those who can read without their fantasy history tales as mind filters—the Civil War was fought not *for* a state's "right" but *against* a state's outright "WRONG" actions committed against fellow human beings.

Confederate apologists complain that Lincoln abused the US Constitution and Declaration of Independence by overturning certain states' rights. We'll look deeply into that in the next chapter. What I can say now is that Lincoln made RIGHT a wrong and hypocritical, yet fundamental, statement that was the linchpin to the Declaration of Independence: *All men are created equal.*

President Lincoln realized it was time to step up, proclaim it and act upon it. We are still striving to make all men and "women" equal. It took nearly 100 years to redefine equality to include women getting the vote. Just recently people of unique sexual orientation have been legally recognized as equal human beings.

It's about evolution R.C.C. Time to evolve.

R.C.C.
As for the mind-set that the civil war was all about the slave is a figment of someone's demented dreams,MONEY was the straw that broke the camels back.The federal reserve went against the value of gold too the currency,and the south was taxed too the point of no return,I could go on and on,so........do

some more research,and tell me what you see......fair e-nuff ??????????????????????????????????

HOGUE
Not at all, and the chicken-clucking footprints of all those question marks add nothing to your point. Your historical research needs to get a grip on reality. There was no Federal Reserve in the 1860s. It was created in the next century, kiddo. It was founded on 23 December 1913.

It matters not. Once again we have some defensive white person beating around the bush rather than cutting the South's Lost Cause at the root. I don't prune the leaves of this problem. I expose the crimes of all people at their source. Our crimes like our minion stupid actions and belief systems are "brain-dirtied" into us. We are programmed to commit them without full awareness of what we are doing. God forgive us—or better, let Existence awaken understanding in us—for we know not what we are doing when we are not self-aware, and self-loving.

Sweet Existence, liberate that intelligence beyond identification and conditioned reflexes forced upon us by whatever society has imprisoned a heart and soul.

I'm not personally going after R.C.C., Genevieve, or later Helen. I am attacking borrowed mindsets. I will ever go after the programmed mind imposed by society on us. It tries to prevaricate, dismiss or hide behind its conditioned reflexes to call its crime a virtue. It isn't, whether the prevaricator is Abe Lincoln, "you" or it is "me." A compassion wells up in my heart for you all, my fellow dirty-brained. We need sustained, moment-to-moment brain washing. Our brains are filled with needless dirt from others. A meditator being outside the dirty mind, so to speak, can aim a hose of awareness to clear off and let drop the dirt and grime of ever gathering thoughts and wash away the mud piles of unconscious, swampy emotions.

But back to the evisceration of your point R.C.C., you aren't wrong, just misdirected. It *is* about money.

It's about an economic business model that supports a way of life by enslaving one third of the South's population, categorized as subhumans and therefore exempt from human decency, rights or legal protection. Slavery exists to make money for slave masters.

No slave? No money, honey child.

The Emancipation Proclamation was a noble thing Lincoln authored and proclaimed. He advanced the war's goals to embrace the higher value of fighting to preserve the Union of the "United" States with the emancipation of those Americans living under slavery, thus undermining those who would sustain a way of life based on the cancer of using a slave workforce. All your beating around the bush and protestations against this are simply reflections of a powerless defense of what is, down to its very core, a fundamentally and morally wrong point of view.

***

Now we come to Helen and her outrage matched by the outrages she commits against fact. For the record, I have refreshed and expanded my replies to R.C.C. and Genevieve since they first appeared in July 2015. Returning to Helen's grumpy-old-white-woman rants after they first appeared two years ago requires an even deeper refreshing.

HELEN
Too bad you like to spout off like you know it all. There are still many of us alive who know the truth. Too bad you seem to appeal to the great half educated.

HOGUE
Speak for yourself, Helen. I for one can't presume that I'm fully "alive"—fully living to my whole potential. Most people

walk through their lives like sleepwalkers dreaming they are alive, dreaming they have a soul. A deeper, spiritually skeptical inquiry into the nature of our dysfunctioning personalities might reveal just how dead we are—we dead women and dead men walking, talking, fake living and ever dying. It's good to expose the greatest conspiracy that turns everyone's soul into a slave of ego. The reason being, that once I really confront just how robotic, mechanical, and socially identified with borrowed agendas of others I actually am, the sooner I can drop being a spiritual phony. Then I can begin seeing the world beyond the filter of a socially borrowed and egoistic *flakery*.

HELEN
I really doubt you'll read this as you already believe you're the all knowing all seeing one who can translate Nostradamas.

HOGUE
Your doubt, Helen, is unfounded. I have read you, deeply. I am responding to you. First response: you forgot the "u" in N-o-s-t-r-a-d-a-m-*u*-s.

It sounds like you are unconsciously castigating someone in the mirror and it isn't connecting with me at all because it is "your" reflection doing battle with "you." It's your shadow box, and when you get mad enough to throw a punch, you'll just be breaking that mirror and making more ugly the reflections of your judgments of others.

HELEN
But all predictions can be subject to change because of the human free will.

HOGUE
That's what I've been saying since I published my first book in 1987 and that understanding appears in many of in the last 600 articles and 31 books and counting.

[UPDATE: 23 September 2017. *The current tally is 44 books—including this one—and over 1,000 articles and counting.*]

HELEN
Facts: 1: The black African were abducted & sold by their own African people (including the illustrious Obama ancestors) & brought over on ships to large ports like New Orleans therefore putting the slaves close to farmers who would be happy to have cheap labor there not being much profit in raising food. Being a farmer is a grueling risky business dependent on many things especially weather & a good crop. Not always a certainty.

HOGUE
OK, Helen, let's look at your "facts," starting with Obama's ancestors, the Luo tribe, who dwelled in what we call modern Kenya. They were not involved in the slave trade to the Americas. The African tribes who were involved all came from the faraway Western African coastal regions on the other side of the continent. At times white slave traders oversaw the raids and capture of black slaves, thus it was not solely a crime committed by black on black African. The three centuries of white demand for slave trading from the sixteenth into the nineteenth century was the catalyst for the black slave trade existing. That demand supplied millions of abducted and tortured human beings and spawned all the tribal wars white men's greed for cheep slave labor prompted.

The facts show none of us American white people, Helen or me, can toss the blame of our American society's crime on more aggressive African tribes predating the weaker, more peaceful tribes, selling their slaves to the whites for a one-way trip, naked and afraid, in a piss, barf and shit saturated hell-hold of a slave ship. Next stop, slavery, a loss of freedom, supply and demand at its darkest black and whiteness.

White Americans *demanded*, and African raiders *supplied* living stock to support our white cracker crime against humanity. The whites didn't ask these people to come to Louisiana slave markets to be sold.

Helen, you almost make it sound like slavery was some good favor done to help poor white farmers cut hiring costs by using human chattel—as if this was some virtuous move. Those poor farmers, let's help them out.

Now let's take Helen's words further:

"Being a farmer is a grueling risky business dependent on many things especially weather & a good crop. Not always a certainty."

Yes, ma'am but at least we got our niggers to work the fields on our plantations, they're in our chain gangs building our southern railroads, working in our southern milling factories from New Orleans to Wilmington NC. Farming can be uncertain but our labor force is steady because y'all "chain" them slaves to their work, so to speak.

There are advantages. We got no trouble with labor unions. No worker's rights. Heck! They're not even as bothersome to deal with as indentured white laborers in the North used to be. You had to let them go once they'd fulfilled an agreed to time of labor and service. Not our niggers. They're property, not people. And whatever we beat and work out of them profits the white race of the genteel South.

HELEN
[Fact] 2. The War between the states was never about slavery! That was the public statement just like the drivel the news media gives out now.

HOGUE
Again, if there were no slaves in the South and the southern white population had been around three million people larger to work the fields, there would have been no tension between

BEYOND ALT-RIGHT AND ALT-LEFT: A PARTY OF AMERICANS

the North and the South. Northern heavy industry and the Southern "king cotton" did not compete with each other. Both exported their unique goods to the world and the South was the chief exporter of cotton in the world—including exports to the Northern states.

Where is the states' rights controversy if there had been no slaves working the fields of the South?

No slaves? No Mason-Dixon line to plot out future states as "slave" or "free." No Yankee Abolitionists. No Lincoln elected. No question against any state's right to have a paid labor force of European laborers like any other, and finally, no reason to disunite the *United* States, fighting a civil war.

HELEN
Those so-called share-cropping boys fought the Federal control being forced on them by the north. The north had industry but not farmland. The south had farms therefore the food the north wanted.

HOGUE
Helen, do you believe Pennsylvania had no farmland? Wisconsin? New York? Minnesota? I've read the diaries of many a Confederate soldier during their deepest invasion of the North in the summer of 1863 marveling and feasting on the unbelievable cornucopia of Pennsylvanian farms they raided on their way to defeat at Gettysburg.

Why were the Southern solders generally gaunt and lean and getting leaner as the war dragged on when the Union soldiers only got better nourished as hostilities continued? The fact is, those tightening belts of Confederate soldiers and civilians were in part the result of America's breadbasket, the Northern states, cutting off their exports to the South when the war started and blockading the Confederacy's seaports so they couldn't get food stores imported from elsewhere.

If your statement, "The south had farms therefore the food the north wanted," wasn't a cracked corn fantasy, the South should have amply fed itself throughout the war and the Northerners would have been the blue-coated scarecrows rifling for food in the bedrolls of the Confederate dead. The main export of the South was "King Cotton" not food stuffs. A lion's share of the arable land went to growing cotton, Helen.

If you are going to make this a civil war over food exports you'd get an F in history in the classes I attended when the education system wasn't so, let's say "simplified" for simpletons. But please, don't stop there, go on... Next I'm thinking you might believe Lincoln really was a vampire slayer, because Hollywood movies and comics playing journalists seem to be your next source of "fact."

HELEN
Lincoln knew the truth of the war but knew that would not give the northern boys a reason to fight. He had to have a reason that would sound good. The powerful ones that convinced Lincoln to act are part of the same group today still trying to start WWIII. I would have thought as much as you know you might have figured that out.

HOGUE
So, what you're saying is that Lincoln conned the Yankee soldiers into taking up the abolitionist cause so they could raid the South and recover the food the agriculturally barren but industrially rampant Northern states needed to survive. Adolf Hitler in 1941 might have invaded the Soviet Union for that reason but not Abe Lincoln.

My bullshit meter is sensitive when it comes to people presenting the brain dirt of revisionist history websites and conspiracy bloggers trying to reshape the past to seduce a willingly lazy intellect in the present.

Helen, what you write in the following is a sad example of that.

HELEN
Lincoln was murdered by that same group when he refused to put the U.S. In debt by borrowing & paying interest to support the cost of the war. Until then the country had no debt. There's been debt & interest paid ever since that stupid war.

HOGUE
"Sic semper tyrannis! (Ever thus to tyrants!) The South is avenged!" cried John Wilkes Booth after putting a bullet into President Lincoln's brain.

He made it abundantly clear why he shot Abraham Lincoln, so please don't bring anti-Semitic conspiracy theorists into this debate. It wasn't the Rothschild's or a Jewish banker or Bilderberg cabal, it was just Mr. Booth, a white supremacist and southern racist taking revenge on Lincoln as the war was ending, because the president had defeated the South's way of life, which was sustained by slavery.

Now to the debt question. It's obvious Helen has never read the history of US war debts and how the Civil War debt was paid off quickly by the rapid economic growth caused by the great move westward of millions of American settlers. She probably got her information from the same place R.C.C. bought that bull about the Federal Reserve existing a century earlier than it actually did, giving Lincoln bad financial woes. But Helen's "Fact 3" assembling an apologia for slavery takes the grits and cornpone.

HELEN
[Fact] 3. Not all slaves were abused or mistreated. Many were treated like family & some plantation owners provided them

with education & health care & some were even given small plots of land.

HOGUE
Sounds great, Helen. Why don't you become a "house nigger" and gain an education, health care, and be embraced by a new and loving "family" who love you soooo much they won't let you leave home?

What you say is true to a certain extent, as true as some Jews were treated like family—"family help" that is—when some served as slaves in the service of SS concentration camp officers as family help.

Helen, your observation reminds me of female Jewish concentration camp victims who were "treated like family"— giving "comfort."

Comfort women actually—easing the sexual needs of those SS officers and guards working on the death camps, as the song "I've been workin' on the railroad goes: ...All the live-long day/I've been workin' in the death camps just to turn folks ashes gray/Don't you see the smoke stack blowin'/Rise up to blot the early morn?/Can't you hear the SS captain, 'get these pris-ners shorn...'

Someone's in the kitchen with Dinah (Morgenstern, that is.)
Someone's in the kitchen I know—oh—oh—oh!
Someone's in the kitchen scaring Dinahhh...
ACHTUNG! Dinah blow my horn...!
Dina won't you blow... Dinah won't you blow... Dinah you VILL blow mein hor-hor-horn!
"Please, my honey child, my honey dewed, honey Jew. First dust the ash off my SS uniform coat and change into something *more comfortable* until I have no more use for you."

Helen, did you know that some concentration camps like Theresienstadt at first put on a show to temporarily placate the Red Cross and deceive the Allies about what Nazis were doing to the European Jews during the war? I've seen the movies the Nazi Propaganda Ministry made showing "gentle" SS guards giving Jews small plots of land for vegetable gardens. They let them form art classes, schools. It looked like they got great medical care too from the kindly SS doctors (when they weren't being dissected in experiments). Just one thing they couldn't get—freedom.

Just like your black slaves who were "treated as family."

How would you get along with being a slave of "your" family, Helen?

I'll grant you this, some prisons are nicer than others. Good for them. But a prison is a prison. A society that keeps you under bondage, even as a "slap-happy" slave," is evil.

You can't get around this evil with your rationalizations.

And where's your Christian heart?

I keep hearing how the South during the war was so religious. They were certainly pious about everything but "doing unto others," such as their niggers, as they would have had done unto themselves.

Oh, but there I go again, forgetting that black people aren't "people."

Just like Jews aren't "Aryans."

It doesn't surprise me that southern white supremacists wave Nazi flags alongside their Confederate flags. I mean, the KKK guys in sheets harbor fond memories of the genteel old days, gone with the wind of civil war when they were a "master race" with a similarly and "lame"-fully employed and terrified slave labor work force that would have made Uncle Adolf proud.

We white folk can be kind to our dogs and cats—or even sometimes a few of our niggers that we fancy, like pets.

We're so generous as you say because we can ship people in chains all the way from Africa just to put 'em close to white farmers in Louisiana so they kin git "hep" in the fields because farmin' is a grooolin' and "risky" business.

Bless their hearts.

HELEN

It's just the way man is. Many men considered their wives as baby factories to have the children so they can work on the farms. Some are loving & caring & some are mean & abusive. Just as some husbands consider their wives & children as chattel & abuse them & make slaves of them even today.

HOGUE

I hope you aren't speaking from direct experience here. If you are, you have my sympathy.

HELEN

It's too bad so many (like you) have not lived longer & known true history. I would guess you were educated after the "dumbing down of American" students started.

HOGUE

When I went to middle and high school in the 1960s and early 1970s, it was before the dumb down began in the mid-1970s, even though I found the school curriculum of those days unsatisfactory. The truth is, no education system can force you to learn basic research and study skills. One has to have the capacity, and, if you're lucky—and it seems I was far luckier than Helen—you get your intelligence further sharpened by great teachers along the way who train your critical-thinking mental muscles.

I've been blessed to sit at the feet of great teachers. Thank you Dan Fichtner, Roger Schaefer, Alan Freeman, and so many more.

I had the greater luck to move beyond intellectual teachers to a teacher of the soul. I sat before wisdom and love incarnate, when in India. With Osho I was reborn into a whole deeper "opening." I started seeing and experiencing reality rather than thinking about it. I've caught glimpses of what it could be like to live ecstatically beyond thoughts rattling the cage that is *mind*.

There is so much beauty and joy, infinitely possible when a reawakening, innocent intelligence can begin perceiving and dissolving the societal, political and religious barriers of conditioned bunk.

I can't be trapped where Helen is trapped now, even though what is awakening in me is exactly her birthright too. We're all birds in cages with the door unlocked and open, sitting on our perches crying "freedom!" but the mind never let's fly through the open door.

In the moments without that mind—you can try.

HELEN
You're smart but your opinions & translations are colored by your own prejudices & background. And you're quite opinionated & rigid so no one can change your mind. Too bad. I feel sorry for you that you think you know it all & still have so much to learn.

HOGUE
In the end, we all live beyond or suffer the consequences of our borrowed and unconscious opinions, biases and prejudices. The difference between my prejudices and background with Helen's is really a very small, atomic difference. The difference is this: I am beginning to look at my own ego, prejudices and conditioned background. Helen hasn't started looking yet.

I am reminded of what is possible when one begins looking. I recall these words from Osho. These words of insight could help Helen and I look clearly and completely beyond the filter of judging minds:

It is one of the basics of human understanding that if you want to see the others as they are you have to be utterly empty, without any prejudices, without any preconceived ideas, without any judgmental attitudes.

Nobody ordinarily sees people as they are. They see them as they can. They see them through a thick barrier of their own mind, of their own conditionings. Unless you are capable of seeing... In pure seeing, Philosia, you don't have anything to project from your side, you don't have any color to give to the object of your observation. Then only are you capable of seeing things, people, as they are in themselves.

Osho (1987) *The Great Pilgrimage: From Here to Here*

The truth of this will be borne out by how me and Helen live out our lives. The first challenge is to see whether we are really living—truly open and "alive." Meditation can help. If you, Helen, or any of those hundreds of thousands reading these interchanges, resonate deep inside with what I'm sharing and especially if you feel deeply moved by what Osho just said, the next step is to move beyond words and plunge deep into the secret elixir of life that is the science of self-observation—Meditation.

I invite you to contact me at hoguebulletin@hogueprophecy.com. Put one word in your email: Meditation. I will then freely share with you links, leads and information about the meditation techniques Osho has taught me to help me discover the difference between the golden, moment-to-moment real aliveness versus the fool's gold coating of ego that society teaches.

We need not be the people trapped in this vast majority of somnambulists dreaming they are awake. We can at any moment leave behind all the imposed and conditioned habits of mind to borrow blind faith and other people's thoughts as our own. Otherwise we may go on dreaming this dream unto death after death and life after unlived life, never knowing the vast intelligence, love and compassion that is eternally possible beyond the veil of ego-mind.

I love you, Helen. I love all of you and invite everyone reading to test what I'm saying and explore these meditations. Do not believe anything I've written unless it becomes your own experience. Whether the near future drops a hammer blow of civil war and revolution upon the American people or not, this moment is eternally inviting us to move beyond mere revolution to eternal transformation.

Revolutions come and go like History's weather, but the spiritual revolution is the only authentic one I know that truly transforms the world, one individual at a time.

CHAPTER SIX
Proof that Slavery Was Grounds for Secession: Just read the First Confederate Constitution

I want to take you back in time and into the minds of the men attending as delegates South Carolina's Secession Convention who voted unanimously 169 to 0 to take a willing South Carolina out of the United States on 20 December 1860. They then wrote and signed a declaration of such on Christmas Eve 1860. Below, in their own words recorded for posterity and stated openly and clearly, is proof that the first secessionist spark in South Carolina that lit the Civil War formed a Confederacy of states and a government that was of the slave owners, by the slave-owners, and for the continuation of slavery. South Carolina was the first of eleven Southern states to secede from the Union in this order: South Carolina, Mississippi, Alabama, Florida, Georgia, Louisiana, Texas,

Virginia, Arkansas, Tennessee and North Carolina. The border states of Missouri and Kentucky were claimed but never under effective control, bringing the number to 13 states.

This document is taken from the following Historical Archive source at Yale: click on the *Avalon Project*. I will be inserting points of clarification under "HOGUE" into this document, we'll call "THE DECLARATION."

***

Declaration of the Immediate Causes Which Induce and Justify the Secession of South Carolina from the Federal Union

THE DECLARATION

The people of the State of South Carolina, in Convention assembled, on the 26th day of April, A.D., 1852, declared that the frequent violations of the Constitution of the United States, by the Federal Government, and its encroachments upon the reserved rights of the States, fully justified this State in then withdrawing from the Federal Union; but in deference to the opinions and wishes of the other slaveholding States, she forbore at that time to exercise this right. Since that time, these encroachments have continued to increase, and further forbearance ceases to be a virtue.

And now the State of South Carolina having resumed her separate and equal place among nations, deems it due to herself, to the remaining United States of America, and to the nations of the world, that she should declare the immediate causes which have led to this act.

HOGUE

In other words, South Carolina in deference to other slaveholder states had stayed in the Federal Union up to December 1860 when North-South tensions over the issue of slavery as a right—human, state or otherwise—reached, in their view, a critical mass requiring this slaveholder state to be the first to leave the Union.

THE DECLARATION

In the year 1765, that portion of the British Empire embracing Great Britain, undertook to make laws for the government of that portion composed of the thirteen American Colonies. A struggle for the right of self-government ensued, which resulted, on the 4th of July, 1776, in a Declaration, by the Colonies, "that they are, and of right ought to be, FREE AND INDEPENDENT STATES; and that, as free and independent States, they have full power to levy war, conclude peace, contract alliances, establish commerce, and to do all other acts and things which independent States may of right do."

They further solemnly declared that whenever any "form of government becomes destructive of the ends for which it was established, it is the right of the people to alter or abolish it, and to institute a new government." Deeming the Government of Great Britain to have become destructive of these ends, they declared that the Colonies "are absolved from all allegiance to the British Crown, and that all political connection between them and the State of Great Britain is, and ought to be, totally dissolved."

In pursuance of this Declaration of Independence, each of the thirteen States proceeded to exercise its separate sovereignty; adopted for itself a Constitution, and appointed officers for the administration of government in all its departments—Legislative, Executive and Judicial. For purposes of defense, they united their arms and their counsels; and, in 1778, they entered into a League known as the Articles of Confederation, whereby they agreed to entrust the administration of their external relations to a common agent, known as the Congress of the United States, expressly declaring, in the first Article "that each State retains its sovereignty, freedom and independence, and every power, jurisdiction and right which is not, by this Confederation, expressly delegated to the United States in Congress assembled."

Under this Confederation the war of the Revolution was carried on, and on the 3rd of September, 1783, the contest ended, and a definite Treaty was signed by Great Britain, in which she acknowledged the independence of the Colonies in the following terms: "ARTICLE 1— His Britannic Majesty acknowledges the said United States, viz: New Hampshire, Massachusetts Bay, Rhode Island and Providence Plantations, Connecticut, New York, New Jersey, Pennsylvania, Delaware, Maryland, Virginia, North Carolina, South Carolina and Georgia, to be FREE, SOVEREIGN AND INDEPENDENT STATES; that he treats with them as such; and for himself, his heirs and successors, relinquishes all claims to the government, propriety and territorial rights of the same and every part thereof."

Thus were established the two great principles asserted by the Colonies, namely: the right of a State to govern itself; and the right of a people to abolish a Government when it becomes destructive of the ends for which it was instituted. And concurrent with the establishment of these principles, was the fact, that each Colony became and was recognized by the mother Country a FREE, SOVEREIGN AND INDEPENDENT STATE.

In 1787, Deputies were appointed by the States to revise the Articles of Confederation, and on 17th September, 1787, these Deputies recommended for the adoption of the States, the Articles of Union, known as the Constitution of the United States.

The parties to whom this Constitution was submitted, were the several sovereign States; they were to agree or disagree, and when nine of them agreed the compact was to take effect among those concurring; and the General Government, as the common agent, was then invested with their authority.

If only nine of the thirteen States had concurred, the other four would have remained as they then were– separate, sovereign States, independent of any of the provisions of the Constitution. In fact, two of the States did not accede to the Constitution until long after it had gone into operation among the other eleven; and during that interval, they each exercised the functions of an independent nation.

By this Constitution, certain duties were imposed upon the several States, and the exercise of certain of their powers was restrained, which necessarily implied their continued existence as sovereign States. But to remove all doubt, an amendment was added, which declared that the powers not delegated to the United States by the Constitution, nor prohibited by it to the States, are reserved to the States, respectively, or to the people. On the 23d May, 1788, South Carolina, by a Convention of her People, passed an Ordinance assenting to this Constitution, and afterwards altered her own Constitution, to conform herself to the obligations she had undertaken.

Thus was established, by compact between the States, a Government with definite objects and powers, limited to the express words of the grant. This limitation left the whole remaining mass of power subject to the clause reserving it to the States or to the people, and rendered unnecessary any specification of reserved rights.

We hold that the Government thus established is subject to the two great principles asserted in the Declaration of Independence; and we hold further, that the mode of its formation subjects it to a third fundamental principle, namely: the law of compact. We maintain that in every compact between two or more parties, the obligation is mutual; that the failure of one of the contracting parties to perform a material part of the agreement, entirely releases the obligation of the other; and that where no arbiter is provided, each party is remitted to his own judgment to determine the fact of failure, with all its consequences.

In the present case, that fact is established with certainty. We assert that fourteen of the States have deliberately refused, for years past, to fulfill their constitutional obligations, and we refer to their own Statutes for the proof.

The Constitution of the United States, in its fourth Article, provides as follows: "No person held to service or labor in one State, under the laws thereof, escaping into another, shall, in consequence of any law or regulation therein, be discharged from such service or labor, but shall be delivered up, on claim of the party to whom such service or labor may be due."

HOGUE

That "person" is non-other than a SLAVE, "held to service or labor in one State, under the laws thereof, escaping into another, shall, in consequence of any law or regulation therein, be discharged from such service or labor, but shall be delivered up, on claim of the party to whom such service or labor may be due."

Again, the division of interpretation between Northerners and Southerners of this Fourth Article divided on the lines of free and enslaved men. Right or wrong, the issue of slavery is the matrix causing this divide, not states' rights. Do not confuse the legal vector with what it's carrying.

What had happened in the North was a growing moral awareness that slavery was evil. In the South, evil or not, it provided the means for their agrarian way of life—cotton—to sustain itself. The Northern states began breaking this compact because they could not in their hearts deliver African Americans seeking refuge from slavery back to the Southern states by force. Yes indeed, the North had broken the compact. And on the grounds of that act of bad Northern faith, and on the grounds of the South wishing to sustain their crime against human beings they didn't recognize as humans, this grievance of South Carolina led to this declaration of secession.

THE DECLARATION

This stipulation was so material to the compact, that without it that compact would not have been made. The greater number of the contracting parties held slaves, and they had previously evinced their estimate of the value of such a stipulation by making it a condition in the Ordinance for the government of the territory ceded by Virginia, which now composes the States north of the Ohio River.

The same article of the Constitution stipulates also for rendition by the several States of fugitives from justice from the other States.

HOGUE

Read "fugitives from *slavery* from other States." From now on, the rest of this Declaration focuses on the slave issue as the cause for their secession. Please read it carefully, especially all those folks who read or dropped a comment or two inserted in the last two [chapters] who complained that secession was a states' rights dispute without going any farther to explain what was in dispute as a "right."

These gentlemen of the South Carolina Secession Convention, the point men of the Confederate rebellion, unlike their modern apologists, have no qualms about spelling it out in writing what they have a right to hold as property, human beings. These human beings are descendants of Africans who had been abducted from their homes, against their will and sold into slavery that made possible the Southern way of life up to the Civil War. Those of you apologizing for that lost way of life apparently don't read your own white ancestors' clearly defined stance as pro-racist, pro-slave. Why indeed do you shy away from this conviction?

They didn't.

THE DECLARATION

The General Government, as the common agent, passed laws to carry into effect these stipulations of the States. For many years these laws were executed. But an increasing hostility on the part of the non-slaveholding States to the institution of slavery, has led to a disregard of their obligations, and the laws of the General Government have ceased to affect the objects of the Constitution. The States of Maine, New Hampshire, Vermont, Massachusetts, Connecticut, Rhode Island, New York, Pennsylvania, Illinois, Indiana, Michigan, Wisconsin and Iowa, have enacted laws which either nullify the Acts of Congress or render useless any attempt to execute them. In many of these States the fugitive is discharged from service or labor claimed, and in none of them has the State Government complied with the stipulation made in the Constitution. The State of New Jersey, at an early day, passed a law in conformity with her constitutional obligation; but the current of anti-slavery feeling has led her more recently to enact laws which render inoperative the remedies provided by her own law and by the laws of Congress. In the State of New York even the right of transit for a slave has been denied by her tribunals; and the States of Ohio and Iowa have refused to surrender to justice fugitives charged with murder, and with inciting servile insurrection in the State of Virginia. Thus the constituted compact has been deliberately broken and disregarded by the non-slaveholding States, and the consequence follows that South Carolina is released from her obligation.

HOGUE

These secessionist slaveholders are specific. They define this state' right controversy as a disagreement between Northern anti-slave and Southern pro-slave states. So why is it that so many modern Southerners keep disconnecting the problem from the state' right?

I believe it's mostly out of ignorance. I doubt that in these days of declining education scores the Northerners on average don't know Jack about the views of their pro-Union ancestors. For the Southerner it is far more imperative to sustain happier myths about the good old, *Gone with the Wind* days before the war. The less you know what ugliness was considered a "right" of states, the easier it is to love your "heritage" based on this "Voldamort" issue, i.e., the "issue" that cannot be named. (Whisper, whisper…s-l-a-v-e-r-y…)

THE DECLARATION
The ends for which the Constitution was framed are declared by itself to be "to form a more perfect union, establish justice, insure domestic tranquility, provide for the common defense, promote the general welfare, and secure the blessings of liberty to ourselves and our posterity."

HOGUE
Blacks, of course, are not "people" in the South Carolinian view of 1860, so the Constitution doesn't apply to their slaves, whereas a feeling in the North grew that those rights could not hold true for all if half the country kept human beings as slaves. Indeed, in the South one out of three people were slaves.

THE DECLARATION
These ends it endeavored to accomplish by a Federal Government, in which each State was recognized as an equal, and had separate control over its own institutions. The right of property in slaves was recognized by giving to free persons distinct political rights, by giving them the right to represent, and burdening them with direct taxes for three-fifths of their slaves; by authorizing the importation of slaves for twenty

years; and by stipulating for the rendition of fugitives from labor.

We affirm that these ends for which this Government was instituted have been defeated, and the Government itself has been made destructive of them by the action of the non-slaveholding States.

HOGUE
This is correct. Those laws of compromise agreed to in Washington prevented the Civil War happening decades earlier than it did. The problem when governance legalizes something evil is that it can delay the truth of evil from hatching out. Eventually, it does hatch out and those laws protecting an evil are broken. America's understanding of people and individual rights was evolving faster in the North than in the South.

I doubt very much that if the North needed a slave workforce to run its farms and factories as much as the South that these rules would have been broken for another 50 years or more. One can go on debating whether the aggrieved slaveholder states were right or wrong in their interpretation of the law being broken by the anti-slave states. What I'm emphasizing here is that all problems that led to the Civil War are sourced to the cancer of Slavery in America. It made northern states break the law in bad faith, and compelled slaveholder states to defend a constitutional law that was morally unjust. In the end, this impasse had to be settled in blood and fire on the battlefield.

What the Declaration says next is true:

THE DECLARATION
Those [Northern] States have assume the right of deciding upon the propriety of our domestic institutions; and have denied the rights of property established in fifteen of the States and recognized by the Constitution; they have denounced as sinful the institution of slavery; they have permitted open

establishment among them of societies, whose avowed object is to disturb the peace and to eloign the property of the citizens of other States. They have encouraged and assisted thousands of our slaves to leave their homes; and those who remain, have been incited by emissaries, books and pictures to servile insurrection.

For twenty-five years this agitation has been steadily increasing, until it has now secured to its aid the power of the common Government. Observing the forms of the Constitution, a sectional party has found within that Article establishing the Executive Department, the means of subverting the Constitution itself. A geographical line has been drawn across the Union, and all the States north of that line have united in the election of a man to the high office of President of the United States, whose opinions and purposes are hostile to slavery. He is to be entrusted with the administration of the common Government, because he has declared that that "Government cannot endure permanently half slave, half free," and that the public mind must rest in the belief that slavery is in the course of ultimate extinction.

This sectional combination for the submersion of the Constitution, has been aided in some of the States by elevating to citizenship, persons who, by the supreme law of the land, are incapable of becoming citizens; and their votes have been used to inaugurate a new policy, hostile to the South, and destructive of its beliefs and safety.

HOGUE

All true. The states have divided over this issue along the Mason-Dixon-Line compromise. Then, the Northern states pick Lincoln, who already is known and detested by the South for including an anti-slavery clause in his political platform. No need for Emancipation Proclamations to put it in writing two years into the Civil War. The North have done the unthinkable, given black men in some states the vote. Black men who aren't human enough to be considered "white" men created equal under the Declaration of Independence and the US Constitution, according to the slaveholder state's view. Everything that led to this Civil War is about slavery.

The Northerners aren't telling you this. Some Yankee revisionist historians aren't overemphasizing it.

I have put before you all the words of the first secessionists to boldly act in South Carolina. They had assembled a more than willing white populace in complete support. The first shot fired in the American Civil War would vomit in flame out of a South Carolina cannon battery shelling the Federal-held Fort Sumter in Charleston Harbor on 12 April 1861.

I would propose that you Apologists haven't honored those men in your defense of their "way of life" as you honestly should. If you did, we'd see you write comments proudly promoting the return of slavery to America. You'd demand all African Americans be returned to your cotton fields.

You don't dare declare that, because this country has evolved too far and shed too much blood in a civil war to throw us all back to the previous and hypocritical definition of *equality* in our Declaration of Independence and the US Constitution.

Indeed many of you still believe that blacks are subhuman, but dream as you might, you do not live in a time that supports turning back that clock. You have not the political or cultural support to make it so. Men of the South like in Columbus, SC, in December 1860, who drafted this declaration, were prescient about what a Lincoln government meant to their future—no future for the slavery-based economic system, the foundation of their way of life:

THE DECLARATION
On the 4th day of March next, this party [The anti-Slave Republican Party and Lincoln] will take possession of the

Government. It has announced that the South shall be excluded from the common territory, that the judicial tribunals shall be made sectional, and that a war must be waged against slavery until it shall cease throughout the United States.

The guaranties of the Constitution will then no longer exist; the equal rights of the States will be lost. The slaveholding States will no longer have the power of self-government, or self-protection, and the Federal Government will have become their enemy.

Sectional interest and animosity will deepen the irritation, and all hope of remedy is rendered vain, by the fact that public opinion at the North has invested a great political error with the sanction of more erroneous religious belief.

We, therefore, the People of South Carolina, by our delegates in Convention assembled, appealing to the Supreme Judge of the world for the rectitude of our intentions, have solemnly declared that the Union heretofore existing between this State and the other States of North America, is dissolved, and that the State of South Carolina has resumed her position among the nations of the world, as a separate and independent State; with full power to levy war, conclude peace, contract alliances, establish commerce, and to do all other acts and things which independent States may of right do.

Adopted December 24, 1860

HOGUE

One final point, the American Historical Association wrote— and with my underline added—the following taking place on 8 February 1861:

Delegates in Montgomery [Alabama] adopt a provisional constitution for the Confederate States of America. The document contains only a few variations from the U.S. Constitution, <u>among which are a clause protecting slavery</u> and one that prohibits tariffs designed to protect domestic industry.

We can't escape fact. We can pretend that ignorance is our shield only for so long. We can hope that someone burns the documents and the evidence that slavery is the center of all things leading to the "first" civil war in America's past. Now we need to look at what might cause a "second" civil war in America's near future. From the battle of the "Blue and the Gray" we approach a battle between the "Blue and the Red" Americas.

CHAPTER SEVEN
Take off your Blue Democrat
And Red Republican
Tinted Glasses

In American elementary schools, a child is indoctrinated to think of the US Civil War as a battle between "the Blue and the Gray" yet the child still alive in me asks why. Most of the Northern states' assembly of soldiers adopted the dark blue coat and sky blue pants of the US Federal Army since they were true-blue Union defenders. Many soldiers fighting for the Southern or Confederate States, however, came similarly attired, causing quite a lot of deadly confusion in the first major battle at Bull Run on 16 July 1861. Union militia units also appeared on the battlefield wearing the standard gray state militia uniform—as gray as a number of rebel state militias they clashed with.

Eventually as the war intensified, both opposing armies adapted into their distinctive blue versus gray fashions as a majority choice. Most of the South's soldiers at Bull Run charged the Yankees crying their bloodcurdling rebel yell dressed in state militia gray, while a majority of the North stood their ground to kill and be killed in blue. If you didn't want to be shot by friendly fire a man uniformed himself in blue as a Federal soldier. A Confederate man wore state-militia gray for "states-rights" secession.

If there's a second American Civil War in the early 2020s, there will also be a color code defining polarized communities of antagonistic Americans. The Blue and the Gray will become the Blue and the Red.

Rather than a "die"—the throwing of one "dice"—being cast, this time the "dye" coloring the next uncivil crap shoot of fate may have already been "cast." *Red* Americans are "conservative," Republican-leaning, demographically rural dominant, separated from the *Blue* Americans, who are tagged as "liberals," mostly Democrat leaning, and urban-dominant.

One thing both Red and Blue Americans can agree on. The division has only deepened under President Trump. I would add that it has never been more urgent that Americans snap out of this politically isolating and collective mindset as early as the next presidential election cycle of 2020; otherwise, the election of 2020 could take on some of the dire character of the election of 1860 just before the last civil war. The first secessionist constitution's explanation in the previous chapter spelled it out pretty clear. The 6 November 1860 election of a pro-abolitionist, anti-slaver like Abraham Lincoln sealed the coffin over the last chance to find a peaceful solution. Five months later in the spring of 1861 there was full-scale civil war.

The Blue against Gray parallel strays from the Blue and the Red in one important, geographical point. A future civil war would not be clearly defined by one region, the South, seceding from another, the North. The demographics are much messier. A Second Civil War in the 2020s would look a whole lot like civil wars fought in the latter half of sixteenth-century France between the Protestants (known as Huguenots) and majority Catholics. Like Republicans and Democrats in today's America, the Huguenot and Catholic French people were spread in pockets all across France.

The difference they shared with a Red on Blue America was a demographic trade off. More Huguenot converts were members of the French elite and princely classes. The Catholic majority dominated the mercantile and lower classes even though Huguenots had sizable populations in the lower classes too.

Though 62 million people voted "Red" Republican for Trump in 2016, like the Huguenots, the elite American upper classes tend to be Red Republican. The 65 million Americans going "blue" Democrat in the same election tend to have an edge in the middle and lower classes. Although a majority of the French Court were Huguenots, the most influential and powerful royals and princes were Catholics allied to the House Valois, controlling the French throne.

The Huguenots fought eight civil wars with Catholics but couldn't unseat successive Valois Catholic rulers, despite poisoning and assassinating one after the other. The last royal left standing was the Huguenot Prince Henri of Navarre. He switched sides and converted to Catholicism so he could be king and bring peace to the exhausted, warring sides.

"The throne is well worth a Mass," he reasoned.

If there is civil strife in America, I predict it would express itself similarly to the French Wars of Religion. It could flare up off and on for decades in localized civil breakdown and riots. There could also be a breakup of the union. Some visionaries have foreseen the country splitting apart into five parts. With that said, it wouldn't be so much a battle of regions but a fight between neighbors.

There could be massacres like the French suffered. There were many massacres across the span of unrest in France lasting over four decades. The most infamous of these atrocities happened in Paris in the scorching summer of 1572. It was called the St. Bartholomew's Day Massacre of Huguenot lay people and their elites invited to the wedding of the Catholic Princess Margot and the Huguenot Prince Henry of Navarre. It turned out to be a Catholic trap, crowding Paris with Huguenot visitors and their leadership to slaughter both. Thousands were pulled from their beds and into the streets naked, then murdered in the middle of a sultry August night, their bodies lying in heaps.

Michel de Nostradamus (1503-1566) had foreseen the butchery decades before it happened on St. Bartholomew's Day as well as many other outrages between Catholics and Huguenots. They were significant prophecies set down by a man who risked his life to publish his history of humanity's future in part in an effort to inform and thus prevent the civil wars overtaking his beloved France in his near future.

Oddly enough, I feel these days, more than ever in the last three-plus decades being a forecaster, that I can personally understand and appreciate Nostradamus' dangerous decision to publish predictions about that oncoming collision. So far, I've only experienced wiretaps. Nostradamus was persecuted for it. Only by the grace and protection of his main patron and occult disciple, the widowed Queen of France Catherine de Medici, was he at last and royally honored 18 months before his death, thus silencing once and for all the threatening confrontations on the streets of his town Salon-en-Crau (now called Salon-en-Provence) from gangs of Huguenot *and* Catholics. Both sides believed the Jewish Nostradamus born into a Jewish family of moderate Catholic converts was using his bestselling prophecy books and yearly almanacs as a propagandist favoring the victory of the other side.

It seems that people don't change inside. Perhaps that's why prophecy can be so "predictable." Nostradamus warns his people about the threat of civil war and rather than prevent it from happening they grow afraid of the forecaster and put him under surveillance. I started my warning of same for America in 1998 and had my phone wiretapped on more than one occasion since. My descriptions of what dangers my countrymen and women face around 2020 coincide with Nostradamus' take on the chaotic French free for all starting in 1563.

The cause of a Second American Civil War would be these "Red" and "Blue" definitions of what it is to be an American soaking the dye of identity so deep under the skin and staining the collective psyche so thoroughly that no unbiased reexamination could work to brainwash clean this mind-taint with conscious and compassionate understanding.

I love my fellow Americans like Nostradamus loved his people. Similarly, I cannot help but write my forecasts in the hope of preventing an oncoming tragedy overtaking my people. I therefore have registered over the years my forecasts. Many of these you've read gathered in this important book. Like Nostradamus, I have presented them to you on the eve of what may become a potential American civil war or at least a kind of chaotic revolution pitting neighbor against neighbor belonging to the world's most heavily armed citizenry on Earth. If it comes, the side one is on will not be clear like it was in the American Revolutionary War. Think rather of modern day comparisons to civil and revolutionary upheavals in Middle Eastern and North African nations. They too are awash in accessible firearms. Think of a second civil war or revolution in America resembling the mayhem currently taking down failing states like Libya, or Somalia. Consider the chaotic, multi-sided and bloody travail, six-years and counting, of a country turned to rubble in the Syrian Civil War.

I don't want that future to happen. I'm willing to risk being seen by both sides as a propagator of the other, just like Nostradamus was. It's long odds that my articles, books, and my radio and television appearances can reach enough people and help them snap out of this new and toxic Blue-Red paradigm that can only end up causing a nation-destroying civil or revolutionary paroxysm. Love motivates me to try. Love always embraces long odds.

This ends my preamble written on 25 September 2017.

The rest of Chapter 7 is a Hogueprophecy article I published almost exactly a year earlier on 24 September 2016, entitled: *Thom Hartmann, take the Next Step towards a REAL American Revolution.* It came out a little over a month before the 2016 Presidential Election took place between Blue Hillary Clinton fighting the Red Donald Trump. This article sets up and includes two quoted passages from an earlier work written in 2014. These passages have far more immediate pertinence now.

***

A reader reminded me the other day of the mantra that progressive author, Thom Hartmann, host of *The Big Picture*, ends every hour-long show five times a week on RT America (the American news bureau of Russia Today). He says, "Democracy is not a spectator sport. It begins with you. Tag, you're it."

I have a great regard for him as well as being at times a critic of someone so brilliant, who even now cannot look at the US political situation as it really is. He still sees it as if filtered through a pair of his blue-tinted liberal's "Lesser of Two Evils" mental sunglasses. He still believes a *lesser* evil called the Democratic Party can remedy the threat to our Republic by corporate special interests. He doesn't yet notice the *greater* evil is that which pretends to be the lesser.

He can't see how corporations have made all living and breathing citizens "spectators" in its political "sport." Moreover, just do the math. In the last three presidential cycles, Big Business money has placed many more of its investments and bets on two successful campaigns of Barack Obama and now Hillary Clinton. If corporations have taken over our government, then look upon whom they prefer to win as your next president. They are exploiting the "evil" of good men, like Thom Hartmann.

Yes, good men do evil, when they let their hopes and dreams blind themselves to political realities. Hope becomes a servant of this evil as it springs eternally, hoping each election the Dems will do the right thing they don't do: turn a fundamentally evil political machine into a reformer grassroots, progressive movement.

The evil of a good man like Thom Hartmann is a hope that keeps him politically mollified from grasping this fundamental fact and as long as he dreams rather than "wakes up" he is just a spectator waiting for a revolution that won't happen until he and millions of Americans begin to abandon this two-party chimera of corporations.

I hope Thom reads this following passage someday, and we could discuss it either on his radio show or on his RT show. I share the following passage with him, with all of you, written and documented nearly two years ago in 2014. It's written to help people take off those metaphorical tinted glasses of denial that have made you good people unintended pawns of evil, be it lesser or greater.

Hartmann's quote is an assessment he made two nights after the US midterm elections held on 4 November 2014.

***

Even a brilliant progressive thinker such as Thom Hartmann comes so close, yet not quite, putting his finger on the problem. In the following, he has beautifully framed what's wrong inside the heads of Democrats. He put this comment out on his RT (Russia Today) show *The Big Picture* shortly after the catastrophic midterm beating the Democrats took, losing the Senate.

Based on the Tuesday night shellacking, it looks like the Caucus Room Conspiracy was a success. But here's the thing. Democrats could have pointed out the relentless obstruction by Republicans. They could have highlighted the constant filibusters by the Republicans in Congress with regular political theater: doing stunts in front of the Capitol building every time the Republicans filibustered or refused to consider a bill. Democrats could have called out what was going on for what it was: sabotage. And they could have made the Caucus Room Conspiracy a household phrase.

Instead, Democrats played right into Republican hands. So the Caucus Room Conspiracy was wildly successful.

Democrats didn't point out the Republican obstruction. Democrats failed to point out the real cause of all this gridlock and they didn't push back on the media whenever the media used the word "gridlock." And Democrats didn't point out what Republican voter suppression and obstruction efforts were really all about. And to make matters even worse, as the New York Times points out, Americans had absolutely no idea what either party stood for in this election. Neither party ran on the issues affecting Americans. As the New York Times editorial wrote today, "Even the voters who supported Republican candidates would have a hard time explaining what their choices are going to do."

Instead, Republicans universally ran on President Obama's inability to overcome the Caucus Room Conspiracy...when it was them who screwed it up.

Meanwhile, Democrats failed to show Americans how they were different from Republicans. Democrats failed to run on their platform. In fact, tragically, they ran away from the president and away from Democratic policies and democrats failed to publicize issues that Americans really cared about.

In 2012 the Democratic Party published their platform. Among other things it outlined the party's plan to put Americans back to work, to grow the Middle Class, to reform Wall Street, to reel in campaign spending and to enact sensible tax reform—all things that Americans support.

Where was all the talk about these issues in the last election?

Why wasn't this platform out there for the American people to see?

Why weren't democratic candidates across the country highlighting these issues and their plans to tackle them?

If Democrats had clearly shown the American people what they stood for and called out the Republicans in really noticeable ways, ways the media couldn't ignore any longer, calling out the Republicans every time they voted to obstruct legislation that the Americans want, then the Caucus Room Conspiracy would have backfired on the Republicans.

While that's now all in the past, there's still time for the Democrats to turn things around for 2016 and that turnaround starts with Democrats clearly showing the American people what the party stands for.

The Big Picture with Thom Hartmann,
RT (Russia Today), 11/6/14

These *are* the things Democrats should do but don't; yet, Hartmann still thinks they will, someday.

It just isn't so. It's because deep in their political core of cores, Democrats aren't any different from Republicans.

That's the step in understanding he can't yet make.

Thus spake my Oracle:

Progressives, if you ever want to influence the future of US politics again, you need to abandon the Democratic Party. Let's face it, they are under the spell of corporate money and influence. They know what's wrong. They know what they need to do. They don't do it because, Mr. Hartmann, *they don't want to do what you're saying*.

Progressives, 2015 is the time when Saturn smiles on you, packing your bags and getting out of this co-dependent relationship with Obama and the Democratic Party. Blaming the GOP keeps you from facing your own peccadilloes. The Dems don't fight for your progressive values, so take your progress elsewhere. Learn the right lessons from the Tea Party movement and move on "dot" organize a new political movement in America that is neither Democrat Ltd., nor the Republican Corporation.

Predictions 2015-2016, Chapter Four:
All the President's Memes
Subsection: US Congress running on American *Idle*
(Chapter completed on 24 December 2014)

ASSESSMENT [from 24 September 2016]:
Saturn did smile on the maverick Bernie Sanders movement inside the Democratic Party that began in the summer of 2015 and put up a daring fight against the Democratic Party Machine. Nevertheless, as I predicted in other articles that summer, the party machine would NEVER let Sanders win.

Do not be deflated and disheartened, Sanders followers—Learn.

See.

See yourselves.

See how you once again drink the "lesser of two evils" Kool-Aid.

Next go-around, start your movement outside of ALL parties. Political parties are polarizing phenomena. Create a Political "Community" of Americans of all stripes who seek to unite on common issues, not on dividing and conquering others.

This is what you can be doing in the next four years to prepare the way for a peaceful Second American Revolution starting in 2020.

My Oracle will be watching you and anticipating your next moves.

CHAPTER EIGHT
Reform Now

This essay comprising the rest of Chapter Eight first appeared in Chapter 4 (Get'er Done, America!) for *Predictions 2013-2014*. These following predictions were documented 10-12 April 2013. I had hoped these suggested reforms could be passed during a period of cyclical national soul-searching that usually takes place every 28 to 30 years when Saturn (ruler of karma) spends three years transiting Scorpio (death and transfiguration). What impacts me, reading this four years later, is that the essence of what my "Oracle" is laying down for reform, beyond a few dated details, still applies to our times and the near future from 2017 and beyond:

I asked my Oracle to share with us in detail what needs to be reformed now to revitalize the American political and economic future preventing such a terrible future. This is the Oracle's answer.

The Republican Party must revitalize, adapt its platform to the realities of the 2012 demographic shift revealed by the national elections of November 2012. Governor Jindal of Louisiana is right. The GOP has to stop being "the party of stupid". The party of fearful whites in contempt of Latinos, women and gays just doesn't win you a majority in presidential elections.

Drop that plan that would have Electoral College choices decided by political voting districts, another kind of gerrymandering that will lock electoral power in the hands of political parties holding onto seats in each state. My Oracle knows why this and many other hostile stances against bipartisan gestures are being slammed shut. Dear, Republican Establishment politician, the Jackass-o-cratic opposition isn't your fundamental concern. The left isn't a threat, the far right is. I see what you see, the primaries of 2014 where many of your bids for reelection will be strangled by the umbilical cord of more far right contenders winning core voters in Republican primaries before the midterm elections even take place.

So, Republican establishment legislators up for election, listen well. Putting up the unyielding partisan front in defiance of the Donkeycrats is pure *Dumbopublican*. If you want to keep your seats forget this strategy, pronto. The corporately financed extreme right wing elements hijacking the Tea Party will vote you out anyway in midterm election primaries of 2014, whatever you do. That's the plan. If you think you can sway the financiers and the hard-core voters your way you must be an Obama trying to woo Senator Mitch McConnell or John Boehner to swing his way.

You want to keep your jobs? Find common ground with moderate Democrats and move the country forward getting done what can be done.

Start with things you can easily agree to legislate with Democrats. Build from there. Do that and you improve the opinion of the American people about Congress. There's no way to go but up, as all of you GOPeons and Donkeycratic legislators are measured less popular in the polls than pimps and communists.

The people want you to get things done.

What's left of 2013 is your chance. Early 2014 begin the mid-term election primaries. If you get the country moving again in 2013, you can face those right *wingnuts* with evidence of solid, objective progress. You'll have a platform accentuating the *practical* and *pragmatic* and by 2014 with a momentum of bipartisan accomplishments. You might as well take that risk, because there's new candidates gunning for your job, armed by billionaires to "hunt for bear" and they're waiting for you down the road around GOP primary gulch to bushwhack you because these folk really BELIEVE what you only pretend to support their very extreme and polarizing agenda.

You'll never have ballots stuffed with your name on them on the midterm election day, unless you do your part to change the perception of being a dysfunctional polarized Congress. You could even shame those do-nothing Democrats and win over the moderate majority. Face the extremists of your party with a majority of Americans having a renewed respect for Congress, for bipartisan solutions. They're truly tired of gridlock and those who promote it won't have an easy time unseating you, if you get off your "seat" at work to initiate politically moderate, centrist, *concent*-tric progress.

For the sake of the nation, there are reforms that reasonable men and women must put aside left or right wing ideology and do:

End Gerrymandering: the manipulation of voting districts to keep career left and right leaning politicians secure in their offices.

End Citizens United: come together and end lobbyist control of the people's government through corporate financing. You need to reverse the Supreme Court Decision that took the people's voice and government away, left, right and center. End money's new power making it synonymous with free speech. End propaganda super PACs financed by billionaires in country and outside. Pressure your legislators to pass a new amendment to the US Constitution that ends this corruptive influence of money and special interests.

End Special Lobby Money: There should be no other lobbyist before the US government than the flesh and blood people of the United States.

End the Temptation of Lobbying Conflicts of Interest: You serve in Congress and then you go home and live with the consequences of your legislation. No legislator can ever be employed in a lobbying firm. This will close an iron door in the face of those of you who vote for your comfy future in a lobbying firm tomorrow, rather than vote for the people's business today.

End the Electoral College: Federal elections aren't state focused. End this delusion. The people vote beyond their state borders for the Federal President overseeing the Union of States. Require these candidates campaign before ALL the American people from Guam to Georgia, from Virginia to the US Virgin Islands. No more wasted focus on battleground states. In America's 21st-century reality, the horse-and-buggy 18th-century electoral voting customs no longer aid the people in a technologically advanced society. A simple majority of all eligible voters is not only enough; it makes your federal presidential candidates value and approach every citizen living inside the contiguous "federal borders" of this land.

End Federal balloting laws chosen by states. Let the states mess with their own election laws for state issues. How can a state decide laws on federal matters? Again, end this state-centric delusion. Federal elections must have unified federal laws. State elections have state laws, but any fed-related law in a state must conform to Federal standards of equality across the whole nation. It's so simple.

End the current lazy man's "silent" filibuster rule in the US Senate. Restore a "talking filibuster". The disputing minority would have to stay in the hall as long as the filibuster lasts in order to impede passage of a vote; banning the use of filibusters on House-Senate conferences; and forcing the minority to produce 41 votes in order to block cloture (ending the filibuster).

At present, the Senate opening sessions in January 2013 fabricated a compromise preventing "silent" filibuster only when used to prevent debate on legislation. Sixty votes are still required to overcome any silent filibuster threat to pass legislation and confirm nominees. It's a good step. At least the silent filibuster won't be used to stop all business from coming to the Senate floor. Still, the compromise keeps the changes alive for only one rather than two years. This keeps gridlock alive until January 2014…

UPDATE 26 September 2017: *the silent filibuster in early 2013 could no longer be used to stall the beginning of a debate on legislation. It was introduced as a standing order until the end of the term in which it was passed.* Huffpost *reported in* Harry Ried, Mitch McConnell Reach Filibuster Reform Deal *that now a filibuster on a motion to proceed could be blocked with a petition signed by eight members of the minority, including the minority leader. In 2017, the Republican majority in the Senate has been playing with political fire, applying the "nuclear option," a 52-48 vote to eliminate the use of the filibuster on executive branch nominees and judicial nominees except to the Supreme Court.*

End bills with pork project insertions or fine print clauses that are off subject. All motions to change laws should be seen in the full light of day on the page, not hidden in a labyrinth of turgid bureaucratic narratives.

End Legalese and measures that read ten times longer than *War and Peace* and *Atlas Shrugged* put together. How can legislators READ massive bills and know what they contain? Write your bills so that every educated American can read them and if a bill can't say what it wants to say without being longer than the 4,543 words in the US Constitution, send it back for editing or reject it offhand.

Legislators should then be required to READ the legislation upon which their vote passes or rejects. You might be shocked to know how few House and Senate members actually READ the US Patriot Act or fathom what it has done to centralize power away from the US Congress to the Executive Branch and how it has chipped away at personal freedoms of Americans, blue Democrat or red Republican, left, right and center.

End private money lobbies in politics. This is the most corrosive cancer in the nation's political future. The American people shall be the only lobbyist to power, not special corporate interests, many of which aren't even American. They influence the American people's legislators, shower them with bribes and assurances of a lobby jobs, protecting this corporate creep into power by pressuring compromised legislators to overthrow citizen-protecting laws and oversight.

So what do we replace it with?

Set up a citizen's tax creating a reserve used only for public campaign funding. Candidates will have to stay within the budgets of public money fairly given.

How do you budget campaigns on public money when the cost of political campaigns on the media airwaves grows prohibitively more expensive?

We the People are the leasers of airtime to the media.

If we the people choose it, we can instruct the leasees to provide free television, radio and Internet time to candidates. All candidates will be given public funds only and there will end special interests spending. Thus ends the limitless billionaire golden baths on candidates to finance lies and propaganda super PAC ads. The candidates will have to limit themselves to real issues, not character assassination. They'll have to prove themselves capable of staying within budget. Exceed that budget and they're disqualified from running even if it's the day before the election. The American people will no longer have public servants that can't stay on budget. They'll have to use their resources wisely, intelligently, to communicate who they are and what they will do as a president, a governor, a mayor, or a state or federal senator or house representative.

End deregulation of the Banks. Look what has happened without it! Your Great Recession!

End profit by Speculation. Speculators don't create anything, they don't promote anything and they collect profits based on nothing. Yet, they affect the real product-producing, goods economy specifically through abstract forecasts inflating prices on food and oil to a point that people can't buy fuel or feed their families.

Stop "futures' betting.

End this. Now!

The Speculation Economy is a major destabilizing factor in all that's about to unravel past the year 2015 because it fakes higher prices to turn a profit while generating artificially induced famines, energy shortages, revolution, fascism and war.

Bail out House mortgages rather than Wall Street. We have not heard the end of this painful controversy. The recent bailout agreement gives 2.4 million homeowners who lost their homes because of banks bungling loans and rushing to panicky foreclosures a measly $600!

The lawyers hired to look at the mortgage papers at $250 an hour earned on average $10,000 per home mortgage case!

You, who have been put on the streets, get $600?!

Senator Elizabeth Warren of Massachusetts pushes hard for a review of this injustice. The $2.5 billion the banking industry tosses out is small potatoes when the industry banks a quarterly profit of $25 billion!

Tax consumption. Even Ronald Reagan's former Treasury Secretary David Stockman gets it. We need to adopt a simplified tax code as well as instigate a VAT tax on consumption.

Tax pollution. Big government is one profligate extreme. Little or no government with no regulation of the people, another.

Saturn the grim reaper of reality teaches that people must be governed. Greed must be redirected and regulated. As Franklin Delano Roosevelt often said, his New Deal during the Great Depression was his diligent attempt to repeat again what frequently had to be done for free market economies: "save Capitalism from itself."

Wise governance gives incentive to earn profit and reward wealth to creators of goods with the "good". Government encourages greater profit to those goods that make "good" the air, the water, the food, the health, the protection of freedom and the good growth of opportunities for the people to be enriched in all life affirming ways.

We have to get over our civilization's fossil fuel addiction. You don't let the addicts regulate themselves. You might as well give them the crack cocaine or the keys to the liquor store. Industrial polluting is like a drug, alcoholism, slowly poisoning humanity and the planet. Addicts die young and terribly, be they individual wretches or wretched civilizations consumed by their addictions.

President and Congress, you *can* find the intestinal fortitude to initiate BTU taxes and regulations now, or reap the whirlwind of runaway global warming later.

Reality Check: like it or not, Saturn in Scorpio says you ALL must increase taxes and government investment. Taxing the rich alone won't balance the US budget. The middle class will eventually have to have its taxes raised, period. (If you're screaming upon reading this, Saturn says, "Your reaction is irrelevant to saturnine realities.")

Make healthy food cheaper and junk food more expensive. Mayor Michael Bloomberg of New York is on a crusade to improve citizen health with a moratorium on selling larger, highly sugared and high-calorie junk soda bottles in New York City.

A completely wrong move.

Bloomberg and our leaders elsewhere should reward greed, not punish unhealthy choices.

A wise government rewards greed along with encouraging health of a nation by changing regulation and tax laws, lowering the cost and taxes on the growth, harvest and manufacture of healthier foods. In a free society, you have every right to choose your poison or your healthy manna from the supermarket.

Equal to being free is paying for the consequences of your free choice.

If you choose to eat crap that turns you into a diabetic-prone fat body with crumbling bones and hardening arteries, shall I pay for it? If you freely make life choices that set you on course for high medical cost burdens for the rest of us, you are absolutely free to do that—*at a cost*.

A "free society" has your "freedom" impacting our "society." Your junk burgers, candies and chips will be taxed

123

three times higher than healthy choices. Industries that manufacture the junk food will be taxed three times higher. Farmers who deliver their livestock and produce to junk food producers will pay three times more taxes.

However, if you grow or manufacture healthy food, you will be rewarded with three times less taxation. You will be given investment and loans. You will then soon discover as anyone who has traveled the world and done the Anthony Bourdain—see the world and meet new cultures by following your appetite—that fast food in the streets of the developing world if it's hygienically prepared is often healthy fare. Like Bourdain, I know this from firsthand experience sampling fast food venders in Europe, Singapore, Mexico, Australia, South and East Asia.

My Oracle now shifts focus from systemic reforms to read the future of other pressing social and controversial issues:

Gun control? Get real. Keep your rifles. Pass over your handguns.

Liberals love symbolic gestures that staunch their bleeding hearts and do nothing to end gun violence. Banning Bushmaster semi-automatic rifles is a big waste of legislative time. Assault rifles won't be banned in 2013. A stricter regimen of security and psychological checks should be passed by bipartisan efforts, though. That would be a good step.

UPDATE 22 June 2013: *The assault rifle "and" closing loopholes for gun checks failed to pass in Congress.*

Let's please get real about assault rifles. They aren't the real killers of on average 30,000 Americans a year. Handguns do most of that slaughtering.

Ban these. Keep hard-to-conceal rifles of all types a Second Amendment right and make obtaining and owning a handgun a privilege.

This is constitutionally viable. No one on either side in the Second Amendment debate on the "right to bear arms and form militias" can deny that the 2nd Amendment doesn't specify *what kind of arms* you can ban or keep as legal, or *what size* your clip, your full metal jacket of bullets *should be*.

Now to Immigration Reform. The great Latino immigrant wave is in reverse. Many Mexicans are returning home because of the recession, leaving behind those with a real stake in becoming part of America whatever the economic outcome. Don't send them home; send them through a process that will place them in the back of the line of legal applicants. Give them the chance to earn citizenship without arresting them in round-ups and in a decade's time after fines are paid and taxes are paid, naturalize them. Moreover, when they begin paying their back taxes, allow them the social services all citizens enjoy now, not after back taxes are paid a decade from now.

Nurture and strengthen US-Mexico relations politically and economically. Mexico and South America in general, are the next frontiers to enjoy an exploding and more affluent middle class as we've seen spreading across South and East Asia. Sooner than later, our relationship with Mexico must rise to as high a priority as relations with Canada, China, the EU and allies in the Middle East.

The US must invest in Mexico's greater prosperity. This is the best way to end illegal immigration north.

Political gridlock begets power gridlock equaling a United States infrastructure that can't keep its lights on. I think of the 280,000 water mains that broke across America in 2012. I think of Super Bowl XLVII in the year 2013. In the middle of one of the most watched sports events in the US, 108 million viewers of the NFL championship football game saw a power outage knock out half the New Orleans Superdome lights. The game was "lights out" for 34 minutes because of a faulty and overloaded electric infrastructure. But hey, it could have been worse. Just a couple of months earlier, a power outage at a San Francisco 49er home game with the Pittsburg Stealers on 17 December 2012 turned all the lights out in the crumbling 51-year-old Candlestick Park Coliseum.

Not long after the Super Bowl brownout, another power outage turned the switch off on the home game of the Utah Jazz versus the LA Kings in Salt Lake City.

Once great Nation? Fix your *grid*! You can't be "great" again without it. Otherwise, I forsooth like Dr. Seuss. Watch the "grid" steal all your Christmases.

With that, my Oracle ended the session.

***

In today's politically polarized climate, there's a false perception that being moderate or centrist is ill-defined, mushy, a "mud"-erate political stance. Eventually, by foresight or blood-soaked hindsight Americans will learn the subtle dynamism of moderation is like balancing on a tightrope. The amount of constant adjustment to stay on the rope is far more dynamic than a quick fall off the rope to the left or the right. The extremes of right and left politics are one-dimensionally inanimate (like the guy who slipped off the rope and fell in a heap in the dirt). Their energy is stuck in heaped and motionless gridlock. No movement forward on a suspended line of progress. No balancing, yet to perceptive eyes the balancer, poised on the rope, if he or she is accomplished, shows little evidence of this dynamic struggle.

In the political sense, there's a multidimensional quality in finding a balance to what is fair and equitable. Common ground is an uncommon virtue, especially when people seek and promote the simple, easy, the simplistic, one-dimensional political right-wrong approach of those exclusively Left Progressive or Right Conservative. A politically successful life for Americans will be found in the middle and it isn't gray or boring or motionless to those who actually live the middle political way.

When Saturn in Scorpio's positive potentials are engaged it promotes "response" ability, a pursuit of the truth. That which works. It seeks that which works through a high-wired balance act sustaining a more efficient and perfect union of its various political factions with the constant adjustment, persistence and determination of a tightrope walker. Under Saturn in Scorpio, politics on the extremes is a cop out, a posturing to avoid the real challenges at hand. Viewed by Saturn, those having an unwillingness to find common purpose are really unpatriotic slackers.

One thing's certain to anyone left or right leaning in America: this US Congress, deadlocked in partisanship is lazy. Being deadlocked is *dead* energy. Even the floor rules of the US Senate grant some shiftless Senator-cum-millionaire from duopolistic party left or right to sit on his fat ass on an expensive Italian leather chair with feet propped on a mahogany desk and just "threaten" to filibuster. This pork-barrel politician need not rouse himself to the floor and stop the legislative process upon a bill he politically rejects, speaking on his feet with no food or rest for hours and hours.

I often think the change in the filibuster rule was motivated more by what Saturn in Scorpio has little patience with: a habit of laziness and unwillingness to work. It views as unpatriotic a legislative lack of willpower to pursue practical, workable results.

A democracy can't long linger in this land if we continue beyond 2015 on the path of laziness, escaping from the frustration and pain of compromise and happily, eagerly taking up the greatest challenge to an American golden future, living by a golden rule:

"Do unto others as you would have them do unto you."

Right now, the golden rule is:

"Those who have the gold, rule."

Balancing the moderate constant of fairness in politics is hard work.

Fascism is easy.

Fascists and totalitarian governments whether they are left wing or right wing don't talk to the people. They have no opposition parties with which to wrestle legislation. It's a whole lot easier to simply dictate rather than legislate what laws will be, devoid of any debate. As Yoda used to say to Luke Skywalker when training him to be a Jedi Knight in Star Wars: *The Empire Strikes Back*: "The Dark Side is quicker, easier, more seductive."

The political future of America hinges on what Americans do to redefine and find a golden rule together before 2015 comes. This is the last time, the last chance to peacefully change course from the easier, quicker more politically seductive stances of ideological polarity and gridlock to a middle way approach. Beyond 2015 if America continues to follow the easy path of polarity, it will succumb and descend into chaos. Cue the Galactic Parliament voting in the dictatorship of Emperor Palpatine-cum-Darth Sidious. George Lukas was trying to make that prophetic cinematic metaphor in the Anakin Skywalker trilogy (Star Wars Prequels). You can laugh at the SyFy geeky comparison but a corporate-oligarchic fascist United States could be coming to your "real" movie as soon as 2021.

"How will I distinguish the good from the bad?" asked Luke.

"You will Knooow," replied Yoda, "When you're calm, at peace passive... hmm... hummm... The Force is only used for knowledge of events, never attack..."

Remember, Luke restored balance (moderation) to The Force.

So can *You*, reader.

CHAPTER NINE
First Gather Together
A Party of Americans

To move you forward I must take you backward to forecasts logged and published in late January 2008 for *Predictions for 2008*, Chapter Twelve. The revolution I speak of was only a seed planted by the 2008 Presidential Election in the mud that was Barack Obama's "change" you believed in campaign. As it turned out, he was just "mud," the fertilizer of manure that is the political mind only talking change but not really delivering its flowering. Just eight-year venting of the smell of seduction, a ripe tidal funk that rendered masses of people unconsciously intoxicated with hope for a tidal wave change in US politics.

My Oracle a year before Obama ran smelled something "different" and saw this man as more talk than do, more "cause" without "effect." To those who rail at my statement, consider this: If Barack Obama had "really" been the catalyst of change you could believe in and made it so, what was the "change" Obama brought after eight years in office to America?

Answer: It was Donald Trump and the Republicans owning the Executive Branch, the Senate, the House and a majority of the US Supreme Court justices that interpret the US Constitution.

It was Democrats after eight years of Obama taking a big step backwards in political influence all around the country's state, county and mayoral positions, while shrinking their hold of seats in the House and Senate to a level not seen since President Hoover and the Republicans ran Washington DC into the ground in 1929. That was the year of the Stock Market Crash when America descended into the Great Depression.

You have your dreams. My Oracle loves you enough to spell out your realities. That's the only place any of us can start a recovery of understanding from. I know it stinks. Mud is good, even though it is dirty, and one's crap-headed decisions smell to high heaven. The most beautiful lotus blossoms grow out of the shittiest mud.

A seed was planted in the mud of disappointment, not just for the Blue liberals trusting a jive president, but also for the Red conservatives, who after eight years of Obama, repeated the Blue mistake thinking Trump was the flaming Red change "they" could believe in.

What I recognize is just more mud thrown over the lotus seed to grow something beyond the Blue and the Red illusions. That's what was muddied up starting in the year 2008, and further manured in 2016. Here then is the essay from January 2008 promising the germination of a new color of flower in our future beyond the Blue-Red standoff.

**

A revolution is looming in the American body politic in 2008. It's not a revolution of centrists; it's a revolution of balancers, of reckoners. It will not come from a grass roots movement, because the current two-party grip on American politics wears *Dumbo*-publican and *Donkey*-cratic masks over a political mafia of the elected governing of the lobbyists, by the lobbyists and for the lobbyists.

The people are steadily losing their representative democracy to a new plutocracy—an elite governing class of special interests. Though a vast majority of Americans ache for a refreshing change in their democratic misfortunes, they may have to wait for a rebellion of the electors within the plutocracy because the electorate as of yet has no powerful voice or means to stage an effective third party or independent rebellion. The Republican and Democratic Parties run the 50 state governments that make the ballot access rules. Third parties and individuals running as independents often are forced to jump through hoops of extra criteria to get their name on the ballot. In many states, there are registration fees and Herculean petition requirements. Republicans and Democratic candidates don't have to jump over these obstacles to get on the ballot, but you, Independent candidate, might have to find hundreds of thousands to sign a petition just to get on one state ballot and there's more than a dozen other states requiring the same.

Those who are already entrenched in the system are the only ones who can break free of it. They've got to have some Charles Dickensian, Scrooge moment. See the light. Foresee the dire state of the future of America revealed by the angel of Christmas Future playing *Politic's Future* before "Bah! Humbuggering" the body politic with a political duopoly. And when enough Republican or Democratic political scrooges turn their hearts away from Lobbyism to Populism again, you will see the next great party born in the coming 36 years.

I call it the *American Party*.

It is not politically Left. It is not Right. It is not spendthrift or greedy, Green or Libertarian. Its party platform is about fair and balanced government finding common ground amongst all Americans. In the end, despite their many differences, this country has ever been a party of Americans.

What do Americans all share in common?

A love of country, freedom of speech and religious belief. A fairness in rights given and access to fair wages and opportunities. Generally, Americans are fiscally conservative yet socially tolerant. Change allied with merit and practical reality. Whatever the differences in religious beliefs, the American Party follows the golden rule: "Do unto your fellow Americans as you would have them do unto you."

The American Party can be born overnight when a dozen Republican and Democratic Senators with 20 to 30 members of the House of Representatives pledge to abandon the duopoly and special interest groups that got them into office. The government will not function unless the Left and the Right come in from the extremes of ideology, making fair and equitable compromises to gain the American Party's voting block to break deadlocks and to move forward. Special interests may have gotten them there, but once elected they could serve out their terms winning a majority of American voters over to their cause with the merits of progressive legislation that brings the government back to one that is of, by and for the American people. If this handful of legislators succeeds in making real change, the people will vote them back into office regardless of what Lobbyism dictates.

The American Party could begin with a conversion of just one future man or woman President of the United States who oversees the Executive Branch of the government. The political climate in Washington DC could see partisan passions evaporate overnight if neither party had the president in their political pocket. A consensus-oriented American Party

President in the White House forces the two parties to work out compromises because he or she will veto anything too ideologically extreme or dictated by special interests.

CHAPTER TEN
End Political Parties
Give Birth to Political Community

The election of Trump and the shocking defeat of Hillary Clinton was a change I could understand: a breakdown of the Game of Corporate Thrones. Jeb Bush "was" the corporate Republican choice. Clinton vastly outspent him, and Trump, was the man who ousted the "no energy" Bush early in the pre-Republican primary months. Later, Trump beat Clinton and her Wall Street blessed, billion-dollar presidential campaign, on his relative shoestring budget of a few hundred million dollars.

In this game of thrones the Lannister "Bastard" unexpectedly took the throne of swords. He's a "prince" of the elite classes but some might whisper that he's a mad renegade. Others might call him the Red conservative people's angry answer to corporations and Washington corruption. Either way, Trump is real change, beyond idle beliefs. One might even recoil in shock and declare him change that's "unbelievable."

Trump, for all his many faults, is where he is today sitting in the Oval Office because the corporate powers that made

Hillary their poster child puppet did not believe a grassroots, popular movement of predominantly white working class people in red states would take Trump over the electoral threshold of 270 votes to victory. All the protests of 65 million Clinton supporters with a 2.8 million popular vote edge could not prevent that change they didn't believe in from happening.

This is a key moment exposing the two-party duopoly in turmoil. The mafia with a two-party, double-crossing, false mask shown to the people is slipping. This essay I wrote for *Predictions 2015-2016*, composed and documented from 22 November to 31 December 2014, is the next important step beyond the era of Trump that all Americans, whatever their political aspirations and polarities, must tread if a bloody civil war or nation-destroying revolution is to be avoided.

Abandon the two-party scam, Americans. The lesser of two evils is "evil" winning anyway. These inhuman corporations are now running wild with their money as free speech, stifling your human voice. They know how to play you. They'll put up a set of presidential candidates who will play "lesser of two evils" with you. Their evil will win because "you" vote it in.

You can't be less evil, no more than you can be less pregnant than somebody else when impregnated. So, you Democrats will use your majority population in 2016 to vote in the lesser evil, Hillary Clinton, even though the corporations would prefer Jeb Bush as their more business-friendly puppet. Either way, they will keep winning, thanks to you.

Abandon the two-party system.

Form an alliance of Americans to find a common ground.

Forty-six percent of the US voters call themselves Independents. [UPDATE 26 September 2017: it is now around 60 percent.] Find each other. Assemble on the Internet and then assemble in the streets, in the town halls. Put aside what the DemaCrips and BloodPublican political hoods have turned you into thanks to their bought media hacks. You're always defining yourselves by what you are against. Rather, define yourselves by what you hold in common, what you share with other Americans.

Build from that.

Wake up from this cursed spell of Red and Blue voting that these political mafias have shaded over your eyes and minds, planted by their televised news anchors and pundit boobs on the tube.

Jesse Ventura is absolutely in harmony with what prophecy says you all should do, vote for anyone who isn't a Republican or Democrat. Go on strike against a system that takes you down as a loser, either way you vote. Don't wait for the revolution to trickle down like Reaganomics on your bothered head. The one-percent's revolution is bearing down hard on you. Its color isn't blue or red; it's a repeat of the "Brown" Revolution of Adolf Hitler—brown as the uniform of his storm troopers. Then, like now, it was financed and pushed into power by one-percenters.

They had a lesser of two evils party to help that happen in the form of the Social Democrats. Like your Democrats they seemed to have your interests in mind, but their minds were weak and their spines were generally non-existent. They also were well-spoken failures like Obama when it came time to forcefully proclaim their achievements when attacked.

If Fascism overshadows this country, all of you voting for the Democrats are as much responsible for it as Social Democrats who let the wolf (Adolphus) Hitler into their chicken coop, because you vote like chickens with your heads cut off. You run around the cage all caught up in your pluck-feathered sentiments rather than using your reason. You just don't see how you're being played for a fool yet, but you will.

It's coming. A grassroots revolution. An "American Party" is going to form a wedge stuck in the machinery of the status quo. Its platform will include the abolishment by law of parties, for they are anti-democratic organizations. When you look at your candidates this corporately-imposed mindset compels you to ask, "does he or she follow the Republican or the Democrat party line?"

You think "party." You don't relate to the "human being" standing before you.

Take those blue and red sunglasses away from your eyes and regard your candidates in their true colors.

To do this you need to form a publicly funded media that has NO corporate sponsors or advertisement. This monster media you currently listen to and watch keeps you distracted from finding out how your candidates tick. Indeed, your candidates can't be themselves to get the money needed to run. They have to make false Donkeycrat and Dumbopublican faces, not their own. They, as well as you, need to be free of the two-party money-politics-laundering system so they and you get real, debate the issues of the people, by the people and for the people.

Establish an anti-corporate and publicly funded citizen media. End all political parties by law. There shall be no lobbyist but the American people in Washington. Declare any other lobbying as illegal. That's first.

The American Party aims to be the last political party because it intends to end parties, end corporate financing of elections, throw Citizens United off the law books, and bring the military home from nation building abroad to nation building this soon-to-be failed state called America.

Your country's future demands you go on strike against the two-party mafia by coming together, left, right and center. Find common ground, build from there. Take back your constitution and your country. You have lost it to special interests, many of which are foreign sourced. Evil doesn't invade with an army in our day, it invades with an army of multinational corporations.

Its soldiers are those billionaires who march to an anti-democratic drumbeat, its enablers hide behind robes of Justice in the Supreme Court.

The future will bring us a new kind of revolution with a synesthetic quality, a mixing of systems similar to the neurological phenomenon where sensations blend together in the mind of those who can hear a color or see a sound. The concept of the bitcoin, blockchain transaction is an idea that will morph into new political and social constructs of the Aquarian Age. From math overtaking precious metals as a new concept of value, watch as well the fundamental power shift as blockchaining spreads to other dimensions of life, empowering individuals over centralized control that will eventually deconstruct the need for borders and national identities. International goes "inter-local-transnational." The blockchain unbroken will unexpectedly hasten the birth of a new global society and global village through the avenue of simple market supply and demand for individual freedom over the centralized state.

Bitcoin will be responsible for a political revolution rendering politics free of political parties. We're not talking about a third party. A grass roots movement will emerge that uses the tools of the Internet to network common ground amongst a community of individuals: I call this revolution the "Politics of the Fourth Way." It's not Democrat, Republican "or" even a third party. All parties are systems of collectivization of the individual. They are prone to corruption.

The Tea Party and Occupy Wall Street were early first attempted failures because they went to the other extreme, rather than organized parties, Occupy Wall Street gained its strength and planted the seeds of its downfall from using, and being used by, crowd psychology.

The Tea Party started as a gathering of like-minded Americans then descended into being a den of politicians in a party. It won seats in Congress but compromised its values when candidates sought financing from special interests that tied their puppet strings.

Fourth Way Politics will find a way of being a *movementless* movement. It has to have a platform of what is possible, what is a shared interest in common with others. Parties will fade away replaced by political communities of individuals. A community successfully sustains itself by requiring that people commit to and share a social contract with an understanding that every member has to find common ground and make compromises to live together. Political ideology can't survive in such a social construct because it tries imposing its view on a community. A political community works to sustain peace and harmony. There's no divide-and-conquering polarity of political parties.

The visions of these changes are still fragmentary before my Oracle's inner eye. They are glimmers of a very different future and our present-day mental limitations can't easily grasp it. I will stand watch and bear witness in future books sharing more insights as the visions of life beyond the current and unsustainable economic, political and social programming kindle their light.

THE END
(26 September 2017)

OTHER BOOKS BY JOHN HOGUE

A SPIRITUAL REBEL'S MANIFESTO:
Climb Aboard the Noah's Ark of Conscoiusness

World-renowned Nostradamus expert, Futurist and Prophecy Scholar John Hogue takes you into the world of spiritual rebellion and personal revelations about his direct, 37-year participation in a new religious movement trying to give birth to a new humanity one heart and one eternal moment at a time.

Hogue will introduce Osho in a new light. He is not only one of the most unique, well-known and avidly read teachers of meditation. Osho is a significant messenger about the world's brighter future. He has foreseen the coming of "Homo Novus" (the New Man). You will enter Osho's "Buddhafield" experiment set to awaken human consciousness first hand from the autobiographical experiences of this author.

This collective awakening is never more needed than now. Human civilization seems poised on the brink of a great unraveling—an era of auto-suicidal acts that potentially threatens even nuclear war, the suppression of democracy, and global climate change catastrophes.

You'll read Osho's prophecy recorded in 1983 that is exactly describing our darkening times today. Such times require a new Noah's Ark to save humanity. An Ark that is invisible, a "Ship" of the "Witnessing Soul." You find a blissful birth upon this "vessel" by tuning inward. Boarding this Ark requires a complete relaxation into let go and let "Being."

"Isness" is Osho's ticket to climb aboard the Noah's Ark of Consciousness and Hogue contends from long and personal association with this master of meditation that the only safe haven is right inside the inner eye of the storm. Safe is the center of the purifying cyclone fast approaching the human race.

The Ark of Consciousness is none other than "You" as you have always been: an awakened one, pretending not to be. You are that loving calm—a quietude abiding beyond the chattering mind, celebrating life and being a light unto yourself and others.

Hogue will show us that even the darkest times can bring positive, world-changing responses. Perhaps the light that we have always eternally been is best remembered only when the Misery Field of human suffering and fear is approaching its darkest climax.

Osho has said, "Just as death faces an individual, similarly death shows its dark face before the collective consciousness of an entire civilization. And that civilization's collective mind becomes ready to go deep into the realms of religion and the unknown... This can repeat itself again; there is a complete possibility for it."

The Buddhafield experiment he created may be that fragrance of love and attention, that climate of joy where modern Buddhas—awakened ones—can be brought out of misery, violence, isolation and fear and in the instant of the present moment can make the new humanity, our humanity.

THE GREAT AMERICAN ECLIPSE
(21 August 2017)
Earthquake and Tsunami

Total solar eclipses seem to trigger seismic events upon the lands and seas their shadows touch. On 21 August 2017, the lower 48 states had a solar eclipse draw its mysterious darkness of 90 to 100 percent totality over four of some of America's most dangerous seismic and tsunami-generating quake zones. They are the Cascadia Subduction Zone in the Pacific Ocean along the Oregon, Washington and British Columbian Coasts; the dormant supervolcano in Yellowstone National Park; the New Madrid Fault Line in Missouri near the Mississippi River; and finally, the earthquake-prone Charleston, South Carolina area along the Atlantic Coast.

If the pattern of seismic activity seen in the Great Eclipses of 1999 and 2009 is repeated in the Great American Eclipse of 2017, then either one or a series of potential major quakes of magnitude 6 to a megathrust of magnitude 9 could happen a week to three months after the eclipse. A second wave of seismic episodes of the same potential magnitude could follow 8 to 18 months after the eclipse. Less frequent but no less damaging episodes of quakes and tsunamis could take place as late as 2 to 5 years after the moon's shadow on 21 August 2017 had touched future epicenters inside these four seismically sensitive zones.

We would also see a spike in other natural disasters such as megafires and hurricanes. Indeed, the United States was slammed by an unprecedented series of massive hurricanes immediately after the eclipse took place. Four days after the eclipse, Category Four Hurricane Harvey inundated Southeastern Texas. Twenty-one days after the eclipse, Hurricane Irma slammed into the Florida Keyes a Category Four storm. A month after the eclipse Hurricane Maria made landfall on the US Territory of Puerto Rico as a Category Four knocking out the island's entire power grid and leaving behind unprecedented devastation. In early October, Norhern California suffered the deadliest and most destructive wildfires on record, burning down 7,500 houses, businesses and 16 Napa Valley wineries just around 48 days after the Great American Eclipse.

The eclipse is over but the coming months and upwards of five year of the aftermath as only begun.

World-renowned prophecy scholar and Nostradamus expert John Hogue will take us through a journey mixing seismic evidence with prophetic and astrological forecasts that will try to illuminate what will really happen, if anything, following the moon's shadow passing over America, from sea to shining sea.

The Great American Eclipse comes at a time of significant astrological portents that not only can bring a life-changing experience to President Donald Trump but also to 330 million Americans.

America is stuck and something has to give. Political fault lines in polarized Washington DC and fiat faults grinding out economic fantasy must rock, roll and rent.

Earthquakes can be a creative catalyst for unexpected uplifts of national attention that rethink, redefine and rebuild America for the better. This eclipse may mark the overshadowing of American hegemony over the world, yet John Hogue will share hopeful prophecies indicating that America's greatest and happiest days are ahead, once American is no longer burdened by being a superpower.

JOHN HOGUE'S WORLDWIDE
ASTROLOGICAL PREDICTIONS
For the Real New Year:
Spring 2017 to Spring 2018

John Hogue is taking the stars back to an "ancient" future. Tomorrow's astrologers will embrace what early astrologers and pagan civilizations understood: Spring is opening season of the natural New Year! Have your parties starting around the Vernal Equinox and continue to celebrate the transition of seasons all through April, Easter and up through May Day.

In the future, even Christmas will be moved to March when it will be discovered that Jesus Christ was born a "fish man" master, symbolized as a "fisher of souls," foreseen by ancient seers as the world teacher of the Piscean age. Two fish tied together represent Pisces. One represents the conscious, the other, the unconscious mind—both are engines of human predictability.

Hogue explains the papal origin of why New Year's Eve is celebrated in the dead of winter. He then takes us through the correct procession of changing seasons from birth (spring), peak life (summer), let go (autumn) and death's fallow peace (winter) exploring world events in the timeframe of seasons progressing in their corrected annual sequence. He will apply his 30 years experience of studying the astrology and medium work of Nostradamus to document highly accurate astrological forecasts—saddled to pure divination—that confounds astrologically dogmatic critics as it accurately illuminates.

This detailed and unique examination by a world-renowned astrologer and Nostradamus expert takes you through a detailed, day-by-day reading of coming world events. First he establishes what was astrologically "born" out of important worldwide elections from spring into summer of 2017 and then

147

predicts the negative and positive consequences coming from August 2017 through June 2018.

Read one of the most detailed and comprehensive forecasts of the astrological significance of what happens during the Great American Eclipse in August 2017. More than this, Hogue prepares you for earthshaking changes that it will herald for America and the world in natural upheavals of the Earth, as well as political earthquakes, the renewed volatility of Wall Street, and the crises approaching for the fiat and global economy.

Hogue's future chronicles can be funny, shocking, even terrifying, but ever original and ultimately illuminating intense times lived in the death and rebirth of an age in ways only he can originally and accurately foresee.

TRUMP STRIKES SYRIA:
And North Korea?

President Donald J. Trump of the United States ordered an unexpected mass missile attack on Syria in April 2017, while he prepared a greater showdown against North Korea if, as he said, they don't "behave."

We have entered a new era of razor's-edged danger, rife with prophetic significance that world-renowned prophecy scholar, futurist and Nostradamus expert John Hogue can decipher and explain.

A rush to open confrontation, heedless of any actual investigation into who gassed who in Syria, is exacerbated by Trump's unprecedented game of matching aggressive bluff for bluff with the potentially unstable North Korean dictator, Kim Jong-Un, who may possess the capability to fire Intercontinental Ballistic Missiles tipped with nuclear weapons at the United States.

Nostradamus, clearly gave short and long countdowns to World War Three. One starts counting when a second cold war has started. That happened with the Ukrainian Civil War and a salvo of US sanctions and Russian counter-sanctions in late April 2014.

The short countdown is upon us. A worsening military crisis with Syria and North Korea could unleash a US-Russian nuclear exchange any time from now up through November 2017!

This book will take you into an alternative universe of facts over hearsay, skeptical inquiry over impulsive, uninformed and potentially history changing, and history "ending" international moves. It will investigate solid evidence beyond appearances and mainstream media manipulation to disclose just how potentially (and intentionally) uninformed Trump's decision may have been to strike Syria, and—perhaps any moment from now, attack North Korea—with earthshaking consequences for us all.

This future need not happen, and John Hogue will consult Nostradamus and other significant seers down through history that present for us alternative, positive choices we can make as we stand at this potent and potentially apocalyptic crossroad in time.

A NEW COLD WAR
The Prophecies of Nostradamus, Stormberger and Edgar Cayce

Prophets, such as Nostradamus, Stormberger, and others introduced in this new and topical book by world-renowned prophecy scholar John Hogue, accurately dated, detailed and forecast the coming of the First, the Second, and perhaps have anticipated a *Third* World War. They never foresaw the last cold war ending in Armageddon; yet, they do predict a new cold war between America and Russia "in our future" would merely be a short prelude to the threat of a civilization-ending nuclear war that no one saw coming. This book sounds a prophetic alarm while there's still time to stop the Third World War from happening. Explore these prophecies. Let them open your eyes wide with an awareness that can yet save humanity from walking, with eyes wide shut, into its greatest catastrophe.

~~~~~~~~

THE ESSENTIAL HOPI PROPHECIES

The Hopi are Southwestern Native Americans dwelling in Pueblos of Oraibi. These are the oldest continuously inhabited settlements in North America dating back as far as 1100 C.E. Up until the mid-twentieth century, the Hopi kept a secret, an oral tradition of foreknowledge—signs presaging an end of an old and perhaps a beginning of a new world. The milestones listed are specific. For instance, they anticipated the coming of white people from the East laying down their iron roads with their iron horses. Later they would draw "cobwebs" of airplane contrails crisscrossing the skies. Then came the "Gourd of Ashes"—a metaphor describing the mushroom cloud in the

151

shape of a round gourd stood on its long neck. The test firing of the atomic bomb near Hopi lands was taken as a sign to share the final Hopi Prophecies to people of all races. These herald the world's oncoming purification either by the fire of nuclear war and runaway global warming, or by a fire of a burning love and conscious concern for the Earth and each other.

Once again author and prophecy scholar John Hogue takes a large and involved prophetic subject and distills it down to its essentials for a quick and comprehensive read that includes the shared visions of many Native American nations about the coming of the Europeans to North America and the death and renewal of our world.

NOSTRADAMUS AND THE ANTICHRIST
Code Named Mabus

ANTICHRIST...

The name for the personification of evil. He's the Agent Smith shadow cast by every messianic Neo trying to save those in the Matrix of illusion. He's the opposite of Christ the "anointed one of God."

The great sixteenth-century physician and seer, Michel de Nostredame (1503–1566), better known by his Latinized nome-de-plume, Nostradamus, foresaw not one, but three Antichrists. Each would be responsible for taking humanity one step towards the world's complete destruction.

This is the hottest prophetic detective case discussed among an estimated 20 million Nostradamus fans around the world. All signs are that we are living in the days of the Third Antichrist. It is time to decode the enigma of Mabus—the third and final man of evil who stands in the way of Nostradamus' most cherished alternative destiny set for our future: a Millennium of Peace on Earth.

This thought provoking eBook will transport us through dark and prophetic shadows to uncloak the man who would be king of Armageddon. World renowned Nostradamus and prophecy expert John Hogue, invites you to use this book as a manual for future-sleuths interested in unlocking clues to a preventable mass murder of humanity. There are indications in the prophecies of Nostradamus that we have Free Will. We can forestall oncoming calamity. We can change the future by changing our actions today and expose the bloody hand of Mabus before his martyrdom causes Armageddon.

FRANCIS
And the Last Pope Prophecies of St. Malachy

In 1139 St. Malachy set out from Ireland on a harrowing pilgrimage to Rome, upon sighting the Eternal City he fell to the ground and began murmuring Latin verses, each signifying the future destiny of the popes. His words were suppressed for over three hundred years by the Roman Catholic Church, yet to this day 90 percent of the saint's prophecies have come true unfolding in chronological sequence in 111 Medieval Latin mottoes, and a final coda, that together hide clues identifying the succession of 112 Pontiffs up to Judgment Day.

Pope Francis is the "Last Pope."

John Hogue, noted Nostradamus and prophecy expert and author of the first major work on St. Malachy's prophecies "The Last Pope: The Decline and Fall of the Church of Rome" (1998), distills this fascinating subject down to the essentials in a quick, yet comprehensive, read focusing primarily on the last 36 pontiffs on the list. These are the men who would be Vicars of Christ foretold after St. Malachy's papal prophecies were rediscovered and published in the mid-1590s.

Up to that point all the preceding 76 mottoes had an unheard of 100 percent accuracy, leading Hogue to suggest these were not written by St. Malachy but recorded by someone from the 1590s hiding behind a saintly pseudonym. Hogue explains that all credibility for any list of fake prophecies plummets because forecasts published "after" the event are always perfect. Unlike the usual fraud, the 36 mottoes foretelling the fates of pontiffs after the mid-1590s remain remarkably accurate, up to 80-to-90 percent. They become clearer as the list counts down to the final pontiff.

EVERYTHING
YOU ALWAYS WANTED TO KNOW
ABOUT 666
But were Afraid to Ask

666 has fascinated, terrified and obsessed New Testament prophets, bible bashers, old-time religious end timers, and a pope-pourri of pontiffs for two thousand years. It's been the Voldemort of numbers—that which cannot be named in decent company—from the Holy Land all the way to Hollywood. Arnold Schwarzenegger on the eve of the millennium's turning got his glocks off, sick-six-sexy with the purported number of the Beast of Revelation in his film End of Days.

It's time to lighten up about this trio of sixes. They get in a lot of trouble and unfairly stand alone for the most demonic number in the world, even though they have company.

666 isn't the only number of the Beast out there. The oldest surviving fragment of St. John's Book of Revelation, found in Egypt in the 1990s, proves there's more than one number upping the Anti-Christ, applying the numerical values of Greek and Hebrew letters to spell out the name of the Beast in The Book of Revelation, Chapter 13—Friday the Thirteenth, Jason style.

The title of my book is both outright and an outrageous homage to that other sinful number we all think about, but are too afraid to ask on a date—sex.

David R. Reuben came up with a brilliant idea in 1969 to author an enlightening and entertaining book called Everything You Always Wanted to Know About Sex, but Were Afraid to Ask. Then Woody Allen immortalized it in the hilarious film by the same name released in 1972.

Now, I'm not trying to pull Woody away from blowing his clarinet with the boys at the Cafe Carlyle on Mondays to make us a Sunday School feature film. All seriousness aside, I do think it's high, holy time all of us with an interest in comparative prophecy study "get down," grin, and bare all the things we're afraid to ask about 666.

So reach out and touch some Kindle Reader and enjoy a quickie—I mean, read this quick and informative, funny eBook all about those devil-made-me-do-it-digits.

PREDICTIONS OF THE LAST BLOOD MOON

The fourth and final blood-colored eclipse of the moon took place at the end of September 2015. It's the last portent of the current and rare lunar tetrad that's supposed to launch what some Christian theologians, such as John Hagee, promote as the beginning of the End of Days, unto Judgment Day. Is there more than mere religiously hyped "sky is falling" chicken-feathered hysteria fanning up a tall tale here? Could the last appearance of a reddened moon mark into motion something that even its chief proponents have overlooked?

We've all been here before with authors creating book franchises anticipating, and pimping, the end the world. There was the Millennium (computer) Bug of 1999, and Doomsday scheduled for the Year 2000. Then came the Mayan Calendar craze of 2012.

In this new attempt to restore clarity to an over-popularized prophetic tradition, Hogue explains that Blood Moon Prophecy, just like the Mayan Calendar 2012 predictions, has significant elements of revelation worth exploring if only someone could clean off all the hype, and push the pause button on Christian fundamentalist expectations.

Unique to this book is Hogue's introduction of astrological and non-Christian parallel visions that often prefigure clearer and more accurately timed signs of history-altering changes forewarned.

Go moon gazing with a bestselling author who exposed the "new age sewage" beclouding 2012 prophecies in this breathtaking as well as concise and sometimes satirical investigation of those who play "Chicken" a "Little" too broadly with Christian Bible prophecy. The sky may not be falling where and when they think it

NOSTRADAMUS: THE WAR WITH IRAN
Islamic Prophecies of the Apocalypse

Never has Nostradamus "come into the clear" like this, naming names, accurately dating events and places outright about a war in the Persian Gulf between America and Israel against Iran. Ships will be "melted and sunk by the Trident"! Is he speaking of US trident nuclear missiles, or, the mysterious trident hidden in the Iranian flag? This war is dated to happen after an interlude of peace negotiations in 2014 lead to the worst region-wide conflict the Middle East has ever seen. Armageddon, perhaps? That depends on accessing Nostradamus' alternative future hidden in prophecies written over 450 years ago. Peace is possible, dated for the last dark hour before a war that will change the live of every human being.

~~~~~~

NOSTRADAMUS
A Life and Myth

John Hogue published the first full-bodied biography of one of the most famous and controversial historical figures of the last millennium. He traces the life and legacy of the French prophet in fascinating and insightful detail, revealing much little known and original material never before published in English.

NOSTRADAMUS
The End of End Times

Read John Hogue's last—and often satirical—word on Mayan doomsday or "bloomsday" and first word on the many other significant and ongoing reboots of prophetic time cycles that a fawning paparazzi obsession with the Mayan Calendar had overlooked and neglected while they are still transforming human destiny.

~~~~~~

THE ESSENTIAL NOSTRADAMUS

Nostradamus, the 16th-century physician and prophetic giant, has a lot to say about the 21st century and beyond. The man who hundreds of times accurately foresaw Napoleon, Hitler, the world wars, and the American, French and Russian revolutions and men walking on the moon, did not lay down his pen after seeing the events leading up to the year 2012. His history of the future continues for at least another 1,785 years!

This is a rare little book giving you the low-down on a big subject: Nostradamus, the man, his magical practices and a brief but comprehensive overview of his greatest past, present, near future and distant future prophecies. It presents for your attention a quick exploration of those prophecies that will directly affect you sooner than you can imagine.

THE ESSENTIAL NOSTRADAMUS WILL TELL YOU ABOUT:

—Nostradamus' astonishing prophecies of the last four centuries.
—His mysterious double life, lived in intolerant times.

—The secret practices that opened his eyes to see the future.

—Nostradamus warned us of a "King of Terror" descending from the skies after July 1999. See who he or "it" was when "1999" hides the real date "9.11.1."

—Prophecies over four centuries old that described in clear detail the flaming impact of hijacked jets into New York's World Trade Center towers on 11 September, 2001, the US invasion and occupation of Iraq and the rise of the "black terror" called ISIS.

—There will be a 27-year war of a terrorist leader called "Mabus" the "Third Antichrist."

—A second cold war threatens a Third World War if it goes prophetically unrecognized.

—Visions of a distant future of extraterrestrial first contact and the human colonization of the stars.

—Nostradamus' visions foresee a 21st century either afflicted by planetary ecological catastrophe or blessed by a millennium of peace. The choice is ours.

~~~~~~~

TRUMP FOR PRESIDENT
Astrological Predictions

Take Donald Trump seriously. He's in the race all the way to become president of the United States. The bombast, the buttons he pushes to get people in a distracted nation talking about women's equality and illegal immigration are primed and fired for affect. We're talking about "The Donald" here, at a time in US history when a New York City real estate developer-cum-television celebrity and multi-billionaire business tycoon has saved away decades of collateral attention for his political close-up. He's carefully stockpiled the silver bars of bad press with the gold bars of good. He's let you have a tantalizing glimpse, year after year, on NBC's *The Apprentice* and *Celebrity Apprentice*, of just how smooth an operator a real chief executive can be. We've grown familiar with his style, his larger-than-life ways all witnessed by a crowning shock of bleached-to-cherry blond hair.

Let me be frank with you, he has carefully collected a fortune of leverage made of another currency more subtle than mere money—the currency of notoriety and your familiarity. A sustained attraction for decades fashioned out of love or hate of Trump, works like a carrying fund payment on a property investment. It's time to spend it.

Donald John Trump approaches completing his 70th year on this Earth playing the Game of Life, gaming it well, doing what he loves, and enjoying himself terrifically. A good deal maker and investor has good timing. It's time to cash in. It's the right moment to raise the stakes in his game, thinking bigger than he's ever dreamed before.

Here he comes, and let me tell you, he's primed and ready to negotiate his biggest, most fantastic, most challenging, most stupendous deal yet: convince a majority of the American people to vote for Trump as their next president.

The stars clearly indicate that the subject of this book can take a punch if criticism is fair. Therefore, internationally acclaimed astrologer and prophecy expert, John Hogue, will pull no punches or deny any positive potentials in this unique astrological study of a genius promoter who may be the next president of the United States.

Love him or hate him, people of all opinions pro or con about Donald Trump will find something captivating, surprising and altogether illuminating in this thoroughly entertaining astrological examination.

PREDICTIONS 2015-2016

John Hogue, a world renowned authority on Nostradamus and prophetic traditions, will reveal the potential, history-changing events coming in the second half of 2015 as this year may be the last chance to begin reforming monetary, economic, and political systems. Otherwise, time begins running out to avoid a disastrous future that might ultimately entail a threat of human extinction from planetary climate change. Hogue will take us further, into the year 2016, and how it could become Year One of a 20-year period of "The Great Unraveling" as foreseen by Nostradamus.

Let that not dishearten you, cautions Hogue. In his most epic examination yet of worldwide prophetic trends, Hogue presents in breathtaking detail a thought-provoking encounter with tomorrow's many potentials, where even the scariest future collapse of old systems of order and centralization can also be cause for the rise of new people movements and positive socio-economic and political revolutions. These and other unexpected reversals of fate and fortune are waiting that may nullify many clear and present threats to human survival and individual freedom that seem set against our pursuit of a happier, and golden, future.

Sample Chapters

An excerpt from
FEBRUARY: Super Blowling the Olympics

JOHN HOGUE'S WORLDWIDE
ASTROLOGICAL PRECDICTIONS:
For the Real New Year:
Spring 2017 to Spring 2018

Mercury enters Aquarius on the first day of February 2018. Three days later is Super Bowl LII. Brace your bellies. Thousands of tons of pizza, dip, chips and salsa, chased down by oceans of beer will bloat a few hundred million Americans out of an estimated billion less bing-prone souls watching the NFL championship game held in the American imperial majesty of Minnesota's new rendition of a corporately-funded Roman coliseum, appropriately called, US Bank Stadium. Christians in the stands will be cheering on the head-banging gladiators and will not be chased on the field by Thracian dagger, net, Spartacus or one too many very hungry lions for entertainment.

Now to the important question: which two NFL teams will be waging gladiatorial combat in that future "Super *Bowel*" Sunday?

Let us consult the stars, shall we?

Mercury in Aquarius is all about opening one's mind to new experiences, such as, "not" seeing the New England Patriots and quarterback Tom Brady continue their near-perennial repeat performance, although the last Super Bowl gave us one of the greatest comebacks in NFL playoff history. Brady was off his game, getting sacked and throwing interceptions against the Atlanta Falcons in the first half. There was no "Gronk" Gronkowski to catch Brady's throws. He had been body slammed by the Seattle Sea Hawks earlier in the season and was out with an injury.

The air pressure in the Patriot team's allotment of game footballs couldn't be fiddled with to help Brady's grip—a bit of cheating that got him suspended for several games last season by the NFL. Factoring having your leader and master quarterback exiled from the field for the first five games makes the Patriot's long fight back to Super Bowl LI in 2017 even more heroic. Then they ran into a wall of merciless defensive play from the hungry Atlanta Falcons in the first two devastating quarters of play.

It looked like the miracle comeback was over. No one ever bounced back from a 21 to 3 score halfway through a Super Bowel game. Halftime opened with Lady Gaga, all glittering in silver jump suit, flying down from the sky onto the gridiron stage to sing while banged-up Brady and the Patriots were nursing their wounds in the locker room after getting their asses whipped.

Maybe it was too much great Gaga; maybe the operatically long halftime shows Super Bowls are fabulously infamous for cooled the muscle and ardor of the Atlanta Falcons. Then again, both teams shared the wait, sweating out the seconds in a locker room underworld. In the second half, Atlanta only scored one touchdown in the Third Quarter. Brady and the New England Patriots, however, rallied. They scored 25 points—19 of which were unanswered by the Falcons in the Fourth Quarter alone. Brady and the Patriots tied the game 28-28 with only 57 seconds of regular time remaining. Overtime play started after the Patriots won the coin toss and first possession of the ball. Brady drove the reeling Falcons back 75 yards to victory, handing the ball to running back James White for a two-yard touchdown making the final score 34 to 28.

You can't make this stuff up for a Hollywood script!

Brady and the Patriots achieved the greatest Super Bowl comeback in 51 championships to date with White catching 14 of Brady's passes earning 20 points off of three touchdowns and a two-point conversion, breaking a Super Bowl record. Brady also broke several single-game Superbowl records with 43 completed passes out of 62 attempts totaling a whopping 466 passing yards. The man who said afterwards that he was having a "terrible night" of football was named Super Bowl MVP for a record fourth time.

Those born with Mercury in Aquarius are said to be natural telepathics. Their quicksilver minds can read your mind like it is an energy field. You may not get away from these psychic referees. They can even catch your thought of pinching a slight bit of air pressure so you can "grasp" universal mysteries when airing out a football-shaped cosmos, spinning just right so it glides into the Gronk's meaty hands for an end zone TD (transcendental delivery).

Why?

Because when Mercury is in Aquarius, people like to work in "conjunction" with others—work like a team—even when they're cheating. On the next great Super *Bowel* Sunday, Americans will wallow happily in their own fat before their flat screen TVs in the Garden of "Eatin'" with Mercury five degrees into Aquarius, sextile Mars in Sagittarius.

I'm not usually good at making sports predictions. Although I "did" predict my team, the Seattle Seahawks, would win the Super Bowl if they first took down the San Francisco 49ers in the NFL playoffs of 2013-2014. The Hawks did indeed beat the 49ners in the NFC Championship held in Seattle. Next stop, Super Bowl XLVIII in Giant's Stadium, New Jersey, against the Denver Broncos. The Seahawks routed

167

the Broncos and won their first Super Bowl, as foreseen by your very biased sports forecaster.

"Go Hawks!!!!" ☺

I will augur this for upcoming Super Bowl LII: neither the Patriots nor the Atlanta Falcons will be playing in US Bank Stadium. The Seahawks will return. It will be a game of Mercury-Martian decisiveness.

Hey Shakespeare, tip your Henry the Fifth and drink after me: Victory will go to those who best work as a team. Those few, those happy few, those blue and gray suited and action-green striped band of brothers with the angry ocean raptors on their helmets. To that happy band of brothers goes that clunky looking, silver football trophy, dappled with their blood, tears of joy and sweaty fingerprints.

Since my Hawks are one of the best in the NFL at teamwork, I am hopeful. Therefore I predict quarterback Russell Wilson will do what Aquarius Mercury-sextiled with Mars does best, make his plays in the huddle clearly understood by all. And my Hawks will no longer have so many rookie lineman offside moments. I foresee a new season with a rapid decline of penalties taking third down conversions beyond a Sea Hawk's reach. There shall be an end to yellow flags taking the wind out of offensive momentum.

Your quarterback speaks clearly and directly. Your line will hold as fast and firm as England's on St. Crispin's Day, as if Russell Wilson was "Russelling" up the spirit of King Harry engineering his own Agincourt: Wilson's second one-sided Super *Bowel* victory!

Thus spake the Pacific Northwestern Nostradamus of most inaccurate NFL sports forecasts.

I'd like to think that Venus on that day of football days, being 21 degrees Aquarius squared Jupiter in Scorpio will render the "opposing" team a bit hung over and tuckered out by amorous pre-Super Bowl reveries. They aren't as sharp as they should be. May they be happily debauched when facing my dark blue, gray and day-glow action green boy scouts from the Renton, Washington, practice camp upon the southeastern Lake Washington shore.

Really, it must be the other guys Venus vexes because the Hawks really *are* bright-eyed boy scouts—Go Hawks!

All seriousness aside let's get back to the future of the world in February 2018,

Venus gets her head out of the hangover, tidies up in time by 7 February to sextile Uranus 25 Aries, and get out of that Venus Aquarius Square with Jupiter in Scorpio. Thank goodness that lost weekend of debauchery and Orson Wellesian overindulging with all the karmic heartburn and weight gain, happened on Super Bowl weekend. You were thus excused.

It's expected that people in the Northern Hemisphere, especially Americans, will drag themselves to work with the signature smell of hangover breath of Pepto-*Bismolian* partiers. Super *Bowel* Monday will remind me of other Mondays from the six months I spent in the land of the ultimate weekend partiers, Australia, in 1988. You always knew when it was Monday. If I were blind, I wouldn't need eyesight. You could smell the nation's stale, alcoholic after breath on any Monday, mate.

Anyway, if I could, I'd block off some time for an appearance on Coast to Coast AM on or around 7 February or appear on television that week because Venus sextile Uranus is the sign par excellence for anyone successfully working in radio, television, sound mixing and public speaking on electrified airwaves. Maybe George Noory and I could talk about the "Last Chance Sextile" as the exact degree narrows with Pluto in Capricorn advancing one degree to keep pace with Jupiter in Scorpio.

After football and the "emptying" of the Super *Bowel*—get back to work, Washington bureaucrats, even if the impossible happened and the Washington Redskins won the championship. Jupiter creeps neck-and-neck with Pluto at a glacial pace to influence by 9 February a confrontation with potential divorce proceedings in the air for Trump and Lady Liberty. There's Jupiter, juggling two sextiles with Pluto in Capricorn and Neptune in that nasty square with the American president's Sun Sign in Gemini. Jupiter's transit over Natal US Chart Neptune goes exact from 9 to 25 February 2018.

Seize the opportunity for sextile therapy. Open wounds to the healing air for a hearing and a healing. Let not the seeds of a revolution in 2020 be sown in February 2018 because this US natal Neptune-in-Virgo boom-bust cycle is potentially handing out the biggest economic "bust" since the Great Recession of September 2008.

Worrisome signs will abound that Trump and Congress really don't know what to do to fix this deep, systemic problem of a broken government, a clueless President and a US population inured by decades of dumbed down conditioning to expect a quick fix. Despite decades of leadership decay, Trump's core voters expect that he and a Republican controlled Congress can wave a wand and create instant employment, a quick return of jobs Shanghaied overseas. Just herd my wayward, good old American job back from China, like the cows coming home.

This dream is Trump voter delusional. The truth must be faced. It will take a generation—20 years—to replace the jobs that degenerated and disappeared in the last 20 years.

An excerpt from
INTRODUCTION: Evil Forces in the Moon's Shadow? Every Superstition has a Kernel of Truth

THE GREAT AMERICAN ECLIPSE: Earthquake and Tsunami

Once upon a time, 18 May 1980 to be exact, Mount St. Helens in Washington State famously blew off 1,312 feet of its 9,677-foot summit. In the next instance, its northern slope completely collapsed in a lateral explosion and killer earth slide becoming the deadliest and most economically destructive volcanic event in the history of the United States to date. Even in such a sparsely populated area, 57 campers, loggers, photographers, one crusty old inn keeper and a handful of seismologists on instrument watch were burned and buried under a pyroclastic hurricane blast extending over the neighboring mountains and hills north of the volcano in a radius of eight miles (13 kilometers).

The channelized blast zone extended the devastation further to a 19-mile radius. It did the lion's share of laying down and mostly destroying 4,000,000,000 board feet (9,400,000 meters) of potential lumber either vaporized or taken down in pine tree forests laid low like wheat exposed to the sweep of some great devil's sickle from the force of the lateral explosion. Rivers a moment before that had carried runoff from Mount Saint Helens' glaciers were soon after breaking out of their banks, choked with uprooted trees. All the salmon in the rivers plus anything else living were cooked in the swollen flood of hot

171

and steaming mud floes that vomited their volcanic gray ruin into the Columbia River 50 miles away.

The total property loss came to $1.1 billion. It included 200 houses, 47 bridges, 15 miles (24 km) of railways, and 185 miles (298 km) of highways. The eruption's ignition was equal to 1,600 atomic bombs with the yield of the Hiroshima incineration. That means seven megatons of the initial blast moved a nearly 10,000-foot mountainside north in a sideward explosion. Before the first eruption spent itself, it pumped another 24 megatons of force in a great ash cloud rising into the stratosphere 80,000 feet, turning broad daylight into night in much of Eastern Washington, eventually blanketing 12 states downwind with light gray ash. I have a jar full of Saint Helens ash on display in my library.

A cosmic switch for this eruption may have been thrown 15 months before. The last total solar eclipse to transit over part of the lower 48 United States happened on 26 February 1979. It roamed out of the Pacific Ocean over Northern Oregon and Southern Washington State to cross central Canada before tossing the moon's shadow off Earth somewhere in the Arctic.

I was in sunny Southern California watching the eclipse live on television. There was a static shot of the Portland, OR skyline looming just underneath a low hanging and leaden cloud ceiling. The overcast quickly faded into darkness with city lights blinking on for a few minutes before the overcast brightened once again to its normal gloom of February liquid-sunshine grayness. The people east of the cloud-blocking Cascade mountain range were luckier witnessing this rare event. For many it would be the last chance in a lifetime. The next total solar eclipse across the lower 48 US states wouldn't happen for 38 years and seven months until 21 August 2017.

The band of total darkness of the last total solar eclipse in February 1979 passed directly over waters concealing the Cascadia Subduction Zone, where two continental plates meet.

One slab slides sideways and downward, curling under the other deep into the Earth's crust, returning to a state of molten rock inside the Earth's mantle. The submarine San Juan de Fuca Plate grinds underneath the North American Plate causing the friction and tectonic uplift that created the Cascade Mountain Range stretching 700 miles (1,100 km) in a wall of snowcapped mountains from Northern California to British Columbia. The subduction of the submarine plate grinds heats and makes gaseous and potentially explosive magma that's responsible for dotting the entire length of the Cascades with 15 snowcapped calderas.

The total eclipse of 1979 passed directly over the Cascadia Subduction Zone and went "lights out" over one of them, Mount Saint Helens. Fifteen months later, the once dormant and near perfect symmetry of the glacier-covered volcanic cone, earning it the title "Fuji-san of America," famously committed volcanic hara-kiri, slicing open its northern slope with a samurai-sword eruption.

This, by the way, is not a fluke. It has nothing to do with "evil cosmic forces" either. There could be something more than a coincidence happening here. This book will show you a pattern of volcanic and seismic events in lands touched by total solar eclipses since the year 1999. There may be epicenters that the next great solar eclipse across America on 21 August 2017 will somehow influence and spring load for firing, right underneath the earth where millions on that day will marvel at the sun briefly disappearing behind the moon. These tightly taught temblors will spring loose a few weeks, three months, eight to 18 months or stay cocked and loaded as long as four to five years before they break and shake themselves out after the moon's shadow had touched them with a 90 to 100-percent dark shadow.

Total eclipses seem to trigger seismic events upon the lands their shadows touch. It happened during the Solar Eclipse of

1999 that passed over Europe, the Middle East and all the way across India on 11 August 1999. A similar pattern of seismically timed events repeated during the Great Eclipse of 2009 that passed over India, the Eastern Himalayan mountains, over China, Japan and all the way deep into the South Pacific to a place off the Island of Samoa. On 21 August this year, the lower 48 United States of America will have a total solar eclipse draw its mysterious line of dark totality over four of the lower 48 states' five most active seismic and tsunami generating quake zones.

The event is already being called "The Great American Eclipse." If those who claim to see the future are onto something, there are more layers of meaning waiting to be augured than meets the wide eyes of millions safely watching it pass over them behind a set of solar eclipse-proof shades.

An excerpt from:
CHAPTER EIGHT: Casting a Light on American Myths about North Korea

TRUMP STRIKES SYRIA: AND NORTH KOREA?

Some myths must first be dispelled, if apocalypse in the Korean peninsula can be averted, forestalling the loss of millions of Korean lives, the loss of tens of thousands of American lives, and the collapse of the world economy. These are the smaller consequences of acting without knowing the back-story. I summon a Korean point of view not entertained or told to Americans from the lowest citizen to the orange spray-tanned *Umpa Lumpa* Commander in Chief by their media.

I define history's military disasters as fundamentally moving forward on false premises. Therefore, with the intention of illuminating what is left out in the thinking process that could precipitate the bloodiest conflict since the Second World War, and perhaps trigger a nuclear world war, listen please to the words of this Korean woman, Hyun Lee, managing editor of *Zoom* in South Korea and a fellow at the Korean Policy Institute. She appeared on Thom Hartmann's RT show, *The Big Picture*, on 21 April 2017. There's no better explanation of the background, or a more breathtakingly informed presentation of how the United States got to this point with US-Korean relations from 1945 to the present than what Hyun Lee presented.

Thom Hartmann started the interview by informing his

audience about how so few Americans are aware that the Korean War, having begun in 1950, has not technically ended. He asked Hyun Lee how does that shape everything that's going on.

"I'm so glad that you brought that up," replied Hyun Lee, "because so many people in the United States don't know about that. And I'll tell you what else most people in the US don't know. First of all in 1945 when Japan ceded colonial control over Korea at the end of World War II, The United States, interested in containing the spread of communism in the region, actually installed a military form of government— American military government—in the southern half of Korean Peninsula, and then installed a puppet leader, who was American educated, by the name of Syngman Rhee. South Korea effectively became a satellite state of the United States. Also, at the end of the Korean War in 1953, it was the United States, not South Korea, that signed the armistice with North Korea, which was basically a temporary ceasefire, where both sides agreed to stop fighting. In the text of this agreement it said that within 90 days of signing the armistice there should be a conference held to discuss a permanent settlement of the conflict and also the withdrawal of all foreign troops.

"Now, this never happened. A peace treaty was never signed. China did withdraw its troops but the US never did and it still keeps 28,500 troops in Korea. And lastly, the US still has wartime operational control in Korea. What that means is that if a war breaks out in Korea, it's the US general—not the South Korean general—that's in charge. The US controls and commands the South Korean troops.

"So, this ongoing conflict you mentioned, is between the United States and North Korea, not North and South Korea as many people like to believe. So then, [with that said], a resolution out of the current crisis, which is the latest manifestation of this longstanding conflict, has to be a negotiated settlement between North Korea and the United States. And it has to include the replacement of the armistice with a permanent peace treaty, to finally bring an end to that longstanding conflict."

Tom Hartmann then asked, "So how did we get to where we are right now with North Korea threatening nuclear war and the US hinting at strikes. It's my understanding that the North's nuclear program was all but scuttled. That [President] Bill Clinton in the nineties had negotiated a freeze on it that was actually being totally complied with until [President] George W. Bush gave his "Axis of Evil" speech [on 29 January 2002]. Am I correct in that?"

I must interject here that President Bush used that pivotal speech to present the short list of the neoconservative intention to use military, economic or political means to overthrow what they defined as rogue states sponsoring terrorism and seeking weapons of mass destruction. This included Iran, Iraq and North Korea with a secondary list of Cuba, Libya and Syria.

In February 2002 I commented that, "The leader of the free world, who has at his disposal the largest arsenal of nuclear, biological, and chemical weapons in history, has condemned these countries as "evil." He has put them on notice that at any time they may face the full economic and military wrath of the United States unless they curtail any association with terrorist organizations, and stop seeking, exporting, or manufacturing weapons of mass destruction." (*Nostradamus and the Axis of Evil*, Hogueprophecy, 1 February 2002)

Up to that speech the North Koreans under Kim Jong-Un's father, Kim Jong-Il, had complied, They has suspended their plan to withdraw from the Nuclear Proliferation Treaty and under the 1994 Agreed Framework, North Korea accepted the US supply of two light water reactors in exchange for North Korean WMD. The reactors, the Clinton administration thought, made manufacturing weapons-grade material for nuclear weapons harder, though not "proliferation proof."

As soon as the Bush administration came into power in 2001 efforts to progress with the agreement from the US side began to go cold. After the terrorist attack on 11 September 2001, in which North Korea had no part, the Bush administration worked to slow down and obstruct the water reactor program. Official accusations followed the Axis of Evil speech accusing North Korea was in non-compliance because of evidence originating from Pakistan, Libya and even confessions from North Korea, that it had gained access to Pakistan's nuclear technology in the late 1990s.

The North Korea regime afterwards explained its public confession had been deliberately taken out of context by the Bush administration. Yes, it gained the "knowledge" from Pakistan about how to make nuclear weapons, no less than South Korea, Japan, Taiwan or other US allies obtain same with no protest from the US. North Korea now had the knowledge like US allies did, but that didn't mean it was actively working on making atomic bombs.

Whether this reasoning has merit or not, I recall well the times leading up to the Axis of Evil speech. It seemed the bullying was definitely coming from the US side on this matter and after the Axis of Evil speech made it official, the North Koreans had no need to keep up appearances, at the very least. The Agreed Framework was scuttled by end of 2002 and by 2003 North Korea withdrew from the Nuclear Proliferation Treaty.

One only has to remember, thanks to it being publicly leaked by retired General Wesley Clark, that just two weeks after the 9/11 attacks, Bush's high-octane neocon cabinet had already drawn plans to take down the North Korean regime along with Iraq, Iran, Syria, Libya, Lebanon (Hezbullah in S. Lebanon), and Somalia.

I would say that Thom Hartmann was correct. The North

Korean nuclear program was "all but scuttled" after Bush gave his Axis of Evil Speech putting it on notice that it was on the neocon hit list. How then could compliance with the US-North Korean Agreed Framework go on? The US administration clearly didn't want to talk any more with North Korea, even though that wasn't the case on the North Korean side.

The Bush administration defining Pyongyang as a target for eventual overthrow was a threat of war on North Korea. Better start up the nuclear weapons program once again as an effort to defend the nation, match weapons of mass destruction with your own nuclear deterrent against the ultimate global hegemon of weapons of mass destruction threatening you. Arming yourself against American nuclear attack has a good basis in reason. Only the United States has used atomic weapons on nations that don't have them. Consider the Japanese cities Hiroshima and Nagasaki, filled with undefended civilians that were extinguished by US atomic weapons in 1945, just south of the Korean Peninsula. So close that some Koreans might have seen the flash when Nagasaki was turned into a sea of radioactive flame. One could conclude by these objective facts that the United States "always" strikes first with nuclear weapons. Moreover, the US officially claim the right to use weapons of mass destruction in any first strike on any nuclear or non-nuclear state it so chooses. The oldest target of this state-sanctioned terrorist threat has been North Korea, roughly a half century before Pyongyang tested its first nuclear device.

ABOUT THE AUTHOR

John Hogue is author of over 1,000 articles and 46 published books (1,180,000 copies sold) spanning 20 languages. He has predicted the winner of every US Presidential Election by popular vote since 1968, giving him a remarkable 13 and 0 batting average. He is considered a world-renowned authority on Nostradamus and the prophetic traditions of the world. He considers himself a "Rogue" scholar because he focuses on interpreting the world's ancient-to-modern prophets and prophecies with fresh eyes, seeking to connect readers with the shared and collective visions of terror, wonder and revelation about the future in a conversational narrative style. Hogue says the future is a temporal echo of actions initiated today. He strives to take readers "back to the present" empowering them to create a better destiny through accessing the untapped potentials of free will and meditation. Hogue currently lives on a picturesque island in the Pacific Northwest about an hour's drive and ferry ride north of Seattle, Washington.

Please visit him at www.hogueprophecy.com

Made in the USA
Middletown, DE
06 September 2018